CHANNEL SETTING DIAMONDS

With

ILLUSTRATED PROCEDURES

ROBERT R. WOODING

Published by DRY RIDGE CO.
P.O. BOX 18814   ERLANGER, KENTUCKY 41018

Copyright 1987 by Robert R. Wooding

All rights reserved. No part of the publication protected by this copyright may be reproduced, transmitted, or translated by any means, including photocopying, recording, or by any information storage and retrieval system, without prior written permission from the copyright owner.

Library of Congress Card Catalog No. 87-091115

ISBN 0-9613545-3-4

Printed in the United States of America

Part ritual, part sentiment . . . .
this book is dedicated to my parents:

                Ben and Mary Wooding

CREDITS

Several craftsmen and women of varying trades have combined their skills to complete this book. To each individual contributor I thank you and acknowledge my appreciation. In order of production sequence: My wife Marilyn Jo for tolerating my irregular work schedule, insistance upon perfecting illustrations, and encouragement to complete the text; Dan Kirk for inspiring morale during the least productive times; The employees of Ric Lohrs Quickprint for their patience and reproductions of illustrations; Robert A. Wainscot for copy editing and improving the manuscript; The talented employees of Alpha Typesetting for organizing the manuscript and illustrations into a book form; And, Robert D. Lewis for expediting the bindery assembly.

FORWORD

There are alternative techniques and tools applicable to perform any diamond setting procedure. Many provide the same results. There is no intention in any of the inclosed discussions to suggest that the methods presented are mandatory. Some variations are necessarily mentioned but purposely kept to a minimum to avoid straying from the objectives. The instruction is programmed to offer concise workable solutions to multiple channel setting tasks. Over time diamond setters will develop their own habits and innovate other maneuvers. The specifics of this reference material is reliable. Each procedure can be applied as it is but would better serve as a basis to build confidence and inevitably increase skills.

OBJECTIVE

This book was produced to clarify mis-interpretations about channel setting diamonds. Acquiring the skill has baffled many fine jewelry craftsmen, both novice and experienced. As a diamond setting instructor I have found that channel setting is one of the most involved courses to teach. The average student can learn the fundamentals quickly but a complete course becomes increasingly complex. Each geometric design requires a number of particular tasks that pertain only to that contour. A procedure to set diamonds into one type of channel may not be applicable to others although the basic principles are similar. The objective at hand is to provide an opportunity for diamond setter's to learn how to channel set diamonds by a variety of means and under different situations.

ADVANCED COURSE

Channel Setting Diamonds With Illustrated Procedures is an advanced edition intended for professional use. The reader is assumed to have previously obtained skills in the use of tools and have basic diamond setting experience. Some diamond setting schools and suggested readings are listed at the back of the book. To avoid personal injury and/or damage the novice diamond setter should perform under the guidance of a competent instructor.

COVERAGE

The text is divided into two general sections. Each are consumed of discussions and illustrations. Section I describes basic channel setting techniques arranged in phases. It should be clearly understood before attempting any channel setting procedure. Also, the instruction can be used as a reference source for actual channel setting. Section II is a series of channel setting procedures. They are presented in a step by step sequence and graduate from basic to advanced. An outline of both sections is listed on the Contents page. Particular subjects can be found by referring to the Index at the end of the book. To conclude the course a number of common problems and solutions follow Section II.

CONTENTS

SECTION I — CHANNEL SETTING TECHNIQUES
INTRODUCTION 3

1 INSPECTION 4
   INSPECT THE MOUNTING 5
      Design 5
      Quality 6
      Strength 6
   INSPECT THE DIAMONDS 7
   COMPATIBILITY OF THE MOUNTING AND DIAMONDS 8
      Width 9
      Depth 9
      Length 10

2 LAYOUT 12
   LAYOUT PREPARATIONS 13
   LAYOUT THE DIAMONDS 15
   MARK THE LAYOUT 16

3 CUT THE CHANNEL 19
   DRILL THE HOLES 19
   TAPER BORE THE HOLES 20
   COUNTER REAM THE HOLES 22
   CUT THE CHANNEL 23

4 CUT THE BEARING 26
   BEARING CUTTING TOOLS AND TECHNIQUES 27
   VERTICAL CUT BEARINGS 28
   UNDERCUTTING 30
      Undercutting Bearings For Round Diamonds 31
      Undercutting Bearings For Fancy Cut Diamonds 32
   SEAT THE DIAMONDS 33
      Seating Recommendations 34
      Problem Solving 34

5 SECURE THE DIAMONDS 37
   USING PLIERS TO SECURE CHANNEL SET DIAMONDS 37
      Using Pliers To Secure Diamonds Into Vertical Cut Bearings 38
      Using Pliers To Secure Diamonds Into Undercut Bearings 38
   HAMMERING/TAPPING TO SECURE CHANNEL SET DIAMONDS 40
      Tapping Tool 40
      Chasing Hammer 41
      Fixtures For Hammering/Tapping 42
   TESTING A DIAMOND FOR SECURITY 43

CONTENTS (cont.)

6   **FINISHING**   45
    REMOVE INDENTATIONS   45
      Filing   45
      Burnishing   46
    TRIM THE DESIGN   46
    SMOOTH THE METAL   47

SECTION II — ILLUSTRATED CHANNEL SETTING PROCEDURES
INTRODUCTION   51

1   **BASIC CLOSED CHANNEL**   53
    Supplement for fancy cut diamonds

2   **BASIC OPEN CHANNEL**   70

3   **CURVED CHANNELS**   79

4   **TAPERED CHANNELS**   87

5   **ANGULAR CHANNELS**   96

6   **INLAID CHANNELS** (Round Diamonds)   104

7   **INLAID CHANNELS** (Square Cut Diamonds)   112

    CHANNEL SETTING PROBLEMS AND SOLUTIONS   122
    DIAMOND SETTING SCHOOLS   131
    SUGGESTED READINGS   133
    INDEX   135

SECTION I

Channel Setting Techniques

1 Inspection
2 Layout
3 Cut the Channel
4 Cut the Bearing
5 Secure the Diamonds
6 Finishing

Introduction

Channel setting diamonds is a means to secure a path of diamonds into a groove or furrow of metal. Diamonds are seated down into the groove and held in place by bordering metal. The diamond setter is expected to manipulate the existing metal to secure the diamonds in an orderly arrangement that follows the contour. The objective is to create an image similar to a stream of water contained within two banks; thus, the term "channel" is appropriate. Setting diamonds in this manner can be relatively routine, but it can become increasingly involved with the introduction of fancier designs and an assortment of diamonds.

Assembling a mounting and diamonds involves a series of techniques. Techniques are grouped into six basic phases: *inspection, layout, cut the channel, cut the bearing — seat the diamonds, secure the diamonds, and finishing.* Neither phase is conducted without expectations of effects that it will have on the next phase. Some logical order is necessary. The tactical format by which the ingredients are combined is the procedure. Procedures vary among diamond setters' personal preferences and the characteristics of the mounting and diamonds. Personal skills are limited and there are multiple designs.

To a diamond setter who has never experienced channel setting, the procedure is a challenging venture. First attempts often prove highly successful if all conditions are favorable. Ideal conditions include: a certain amount of guidance from an experienced diamond setter; a basic design that does not require alteration, or a great amount of metal to be removed; and diamonds that will fit properly. Subsequent trials done with different designs and unequal sizes of diamonds can discourage a beginner's confidence. The diamond setter will at that point either give up and retreat to work only on the fundamental settings, thereby supporting the ego of more experienced craftsmen, or face each challenge and accept mistakes as educational experiences. The latter case is typical of the most prominent and skilled diamond setters. It is too easy to accuse the imperfections of a mounting, or diamonds, when many problems can be overcome by initiativeness.

The objective of this section is to discuss alternative techniques of procedures to channel set diamonds. It is an introduction and a reference source to guide the diamond setter later if questions arise during the procedures section. A variety of unique situations are presented in order to expand on the theory behind each step. Most problems can be anticipated and avoided; however, a combination of circumstances will develop in actual practice. Many of these variables are discussed throughout the text. For now, a clear understanding of the channel setting procedure is important in order to prevent or help to solve problems as they occur during realistic working conditions.

1

Inspection

The inspection phase of channel setting is an examination of the mounting and diamonds. Considerations include the characteristics of each and their compatibility for assembly. A critical appraisal of the materials should be the initial phase of any diamond setting procedure to ensure that the assembly can result in a lasting product. A thorough approach is suggested in order to discover any material defects that could prohibit the diamond setter's craftsmanship. Particular details that will cause deviations from the normal procedure are noted at this time. In general, the purpose of the inspection is twofold: first, to familiarize the craftsman with the characteristics of the mounting and diamonds; and second, to find a justification to either question the assembly or continue with the channel setting procedure taking the unfavorable aspects into account.

There are several things to consider when inspecting the mounting. Three predominant factors are the design, quality of metal, and strength. Design is foremost because it is usually obvious at first sight if the mounting can be channel set. For example, the presence of prongs implies that channel setting is not applicable. The next inspection is to examine the metal for defects such as pits and deep abrasions that could affect the procedure. Estimating the strength of the mounting is important because a certain amount of abuse to the metal is often necessary in order to channel set diamonds. Additional inspections of the mounting include the craftsmanship by which it was manufactured. It is to the diamond setter's advantage to become aware early in the channel setting procedure of any improvisions that must be made because of the mounting.

Another major consideration during the inspection phase, besides the mounting, is the diamond. There are valid reasons to check the diamonds for chips, flaws, and imperfect cuts. First of all, if a chipped diamond is not reported to an immediate supervisor, or customer, prior to setting the craftsman might inevitably be blamed. Secondly, flaws and imperfect cuts will have a direct effect on the setting procedure. A diamond setter need not be a gemologist, but an intimate knowledge to grade diamonds is a valuable asset.

Compatibility is the third objective of the inspection phase. It is a series of tests done to decide if the assigned mounting can be properly assembled. The selected diamonds are compared to the width, depth, and length of the channel. When the diamonds are seated between the channel walls, there should be enough metal remaining at each side to secure them. An image of that, along with the depth where the diamonds will eventually be set, must be envisioned. Doubts about the channel length can be tested by temporarily positioning the diamonds on the channel. Prospects for the assembly of the mounting and diamonds can usually be assured by simple visual comparisons; however, there will be less frequent occasions when mechanical means involving a millimeter degree gauge are helpful.

Inspecting the mounting and diamonds is a preliminary task that precedes the more extensive layout phase. Although the condition of the materials can be determined within a few minutes, its importance is eminent. Many problems that could develop later in the procedure can usually be foreseen and possibly avoided. An experienced diamond setter will routinely make several brief checks and tests to the mounting and diamonds as a prelude to assembling them. Some checks are subconscious and others mentally noted. An attempt is made to ponder and envision the effects on craftsmanship that the materials could have during the advanced stages of the procedure. It is not unusual that an assembly is rejected or delayed at first sight. A little time allotted for inspecting permits the diamond setter to become thoroughly acquainted with the mounting and diamonds.

INSPECT THE MOUNTING

Inspection skills are developed and refined from experience. A diamond setter learns from previous performance about machining processes and the amount of pressure that a mounting is subjected to during the channel setting procedure. For this reason a personal evaluation of the mounting and its craftsmanship is necessary. Inevitable problems can usually be foreseen by conducting a visual and sometimes mechanical inspection. The diamond setter should be able to readily recognize inadequacies and imperfections in a mounting from channel setting problems incurred in the past.

Design

Upon receiving a mounting with instructions to channel set diamonds, the diamond setter is foremost interested in the possibilities of the mounting. Most mountings are designed for specific types of diamond setting. A channel setting procedure can be outlined but need not be strictly adhered to. An introductory example was previously given depicting the extremity of a mounting having prongs to be channel set. That would be an obvious

6 INSPECTION

oversight on the part of a superior, but many discrepancies are not as noticeable at first glance. Alterations to the mounting are common as well as deviations in the procedure, but there are limitations.

Within the limitations some mountings are capable of accommodating either bead, bezel, or channel setting. Channel setting can begin from a solid plate of metal as does many other types of diamond setting, but it requires metal that has considerably more thickness. Since a mounting having a precut channel is not always available, a solid plate is often used. If it is necessary to cut a channel into such a mounting, the diamond setter should be sure there is a enough space to contain the diamonds, and that the thickness of the metal is suitable.

Quality

Inspecting a mounting for quality is concentrated to the detection of casting defects and workmanship. Some common casting problems are pitted metal, incomplete sections, and extremely rough surfaces. Abrasive metal can be finished, but that could require an excessive amount of metal to be removed. Likewise, some pits can be burnished if they are not too severe. Besides casting defects, other former inferior work done to the mounting including poor soldering, filing, and pre-polishing, might also be beyond the diamond setter's control. Adjustments can be made during the channel setting procedure to correct some minor imperfections. Compensating for defectives in a mounting that require harsh alterations is often demoralizing.

One of the greatest discouragements to a fine diamond setter is being faced with the job of channel setting diamonds into a poor quality mounting. Channel setting diamonds demands precision in every technique. The challenge is greeted wholeheartedly with expectations of self-satisfaction. Knowing beforehand that the finished product will be affected by uncontrollable imperfections in a mounting, the efforts to complete the task also will be diminished. It is beyond the scope of this book to elaborate on extensive modifications of a mounting. That is the specialization of the goldsmith or jewelry mechanic. In the event that any of the before mentioned problems do arise, the skills of those specialists should be summoned.

Strength

Appraising the strength of a mounting is essential to a preliminary inspection. Channel setting procedures frequently require forceful percussions and/or pressure to the metal in order to secure the diamonds. This is not always necessary, but until the procedure is well underway one cannot be too sure how strong the metal might be. Some weaknesses of mountings are easily detected while others could go unnoticed until it is too late. A mounting could collapse under pressure because of a weak structure. Frequent reasons for fragility include thin or imperfect bridging supports, extended spans, and a weak ring shank. The occurrence of these conditions and others can usually be detected by a thorough visual inspection.

Other factors that affect the strength of a mounting pertain to the chemical makeup of the metal. These include previous heat regulations and alloy content. The metal in a mounting can become brittle or reluctant to bend if it has been heated and then quenched in water to cool it quickly. This negligence sometimes occurs during casting, sizing, and other processes that require the use of heat. Specific alloy content also has a direct effect on the hardness of precious metal. Metal having a higher gold content is usually softer than that with less. However, two similarly designed rings with each having the same karat gold can vary in toughness if the alloy type of each is different. For example, 14K white gold is usually harder than 14K yellow gold. Heating processes and specific alloy content vary between manufacturers. Because of that a diamond setter can only guess the pliability of metal. The estimate is based on experience with particular casting firms, color of metal, and the karat stamp.

Many problems pertaining to the strength of the mounting can be avoided by proceeding with caution and keeping in mind throughout the procedure that the strengths and weaknesses do exist. Sometimes if a mounting is weak, it is advisable to back it up with diamond setters' cement until the setting is completed. Diamond setters' cement is normally used to stabilize earrings, pendants, etc., while channel setting, but the same can also be applicable to rings. The best precaution that a diamond setter can take is to anticipate the effects that each move will have throughout the remainder of the procedure.

INSPECT THE DIAMONDS

A diamond setter normally has very little control over the selection of diamonds for a particular mounting. This is a necessary business practice in the jewelry industry even though at times it interferes with craftsmanship. The major drawback is that the craftsman is delegated responsibility without authority. However, as a craftsman becomes more skilled and perfectioned at setting diamonds, so does the ability to grade and select diamonds for particular tasks. Such a refined skill often exceeds that of some "gemologists." Regardless, the diamond setter must make the best use of the materials (diamonds) available. The inspection phase of channel setting includes the detection of imperfections in diamonds.

It is not uncommon to find chipped diamonds intended to be set into

8 INSPECTION

a new mounting. This is expecially true in the remount and repair service, although the occasion is not confined to those sectors. The diamond setter should actively search for chips rather than passively be on the alert to recognize them. Ultimately the craftsman is responsible for all unreported defects that are not natural. To avoid interpersonal conflicts, chipped diamonds should be reported before setting to either a superior, or the customer if it is a remount.

Natural imperfections to check for are flaws, carbon (uncrystalized), and on a lesser degree, the clarity and color. These characteristics, along with the range of sizes, should be known in order to prevent problems that could develop because of them during the setting procedure. Natural flaws are positioned in non-conspicuous areas of the mounting. If there is an exchange policy within the firm that employs the craft, it might be a good idea to debate the inclusion of a certain diamond(s). Ideally, the quality of diamonds set into any mounting should be comparatively equal. When a mismatched diamond is apparent, whether it is a better quality or worse, it will distract the perception of the finished product.

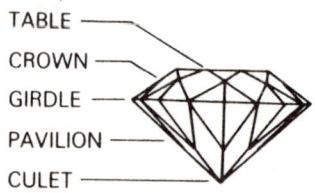

Fig. 1.1 Facets of a diamond

When inspecting diamonds, try to perceive what effect the characteristics will have during the setting procedure and on the outcome. The aid of a 7X-10X eye loupe is necessary for close viewing. To hold a diamond steady use either bees wax tapered to a point, or adequate size tweezers as a fixture. Particular attention is given to multiple top views by rotating the diamond. Imperfections are more readily seen from those angles. If necessary re-position the diamond into the fixture for each observation. Also, examine each diamond from a couple different side views to reveal the cut. A thick girdle or extended pavilion will indicate that the technique to cut the bearing will be altered. Conversely, an extremely thin girdle requires special precautionary measures because it will chip easily. Although channel setting is a unique procedure, the precise method to channel set a diamond is determined in part by the characteristics of that particular diamond.

COMPATIBILITY OF THE MOUNTING OF DIAMONDS

The condition of the mounting and diamonds has little significance if they cannot be assembled. Comparing the dimensions of the materials is the

INSPECTION 9

feasibility part of the inspection phase. The objective is to decide if a channel setting procedure can be initiated that is in compliance with the design. Modifications and alternate plans are considered for tactical purposes, but not necessarily executed at this time. Those decisions are reserved for the layout phase when the precise strategy and related details are more thoroughly developed. Major alterations are also discussed in the phase — CUT THE CHANNEL page 19. Efforts during the present stage are directed towards determining if there is enough metal to adequately channel set the diamonds.

Width

Diamonds are compared to the width of a channel to see if there is a sufficient amount of metal to secure them and to finish after they are set. Critical features are the diameters of the diamonds, channel between the walls, channel walls, and the width of a plate if it is not pre-cut. Most channels for round diamonds are eventually cut to about three-fourths the diameter of the diamonds, although some, such as an inlaid channel, may be a little wider. The channel dimension for fancy cut diamonds are explicit to each particular diamond. In addition, the walls in either case should have a minimum width of roughly .75 millimeters. (These figures are approximate. Personal preferences and each case will vary.) Specifications are thoroughly examined during the layout. At this stage, testing is conducted to detect severe inadequacies between the diameter of the diamonds and width of the channel. The task at hand is to selectively place some of the diamonds centered across the channel, or plate if applicable. Then estimate how much metal will be left after the bearings are cut (See Fig. 1.2). Remember that the procedure can be stopped at any time to investigate foreseeable problems.

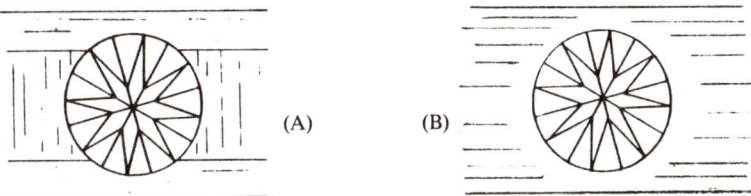

Fig. 1.2   Shows a diamond placed table facets down on (A) a channel and (B) a solid plate to estimate how much metal will be left at each side after the bearings are cut.

Depth

Another serious concern when comparing the mounting and diamonds, besides the width, is the possibility of setting the diamonds to an adequate depth. This can be checked simply by holding a diamond via bees wax or tweezers upright to the side of the metal (See Fig. 1.3). Assuming that the mounting is a ring, it is important that the diamonds can be set to a proper

10 INSPECTION

depth without having the culets protrude into the finger area. A general rule to follow is to envision that the diamonds will be seated to a depth where the table facets are slightly below the surface of the plate. That will leave plenty of metal to allow both sides of the channel to fold onto the diamonds later. Also, if the diamonds can be seated low, the diamond setter will have an ample amount of metal to work with during the finishing phase.

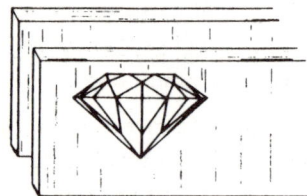

Fig. 1.3 Shows a diamond placed upright to the side of a channel to determine if it can be set to an adequate depth without having the culet protrude into the finger area.

A mechanical means to determine if there is an adequate depth of metal is helpful when a plate is supported by an undergallery. In some designs that do not have a pre-cut channel the actual thickness may be deceiving. It could be high enough that the culets of the diamonds will be guarded, but there is still the possibility that the plate might be too thin to cut the bearings deep. For example, the edge of a metal plate is typically built up more than the center. Economic reasons are given for this deception. Since it is a usual and acceptable means of manufacturing jewelry, the diamond setter should be accustomed to measuring the thickness of metal with a millimeter degree gauge. Whenever there is any doubt, it is a good practice to take a few moments to mechanically compare the dimensions of the metal to the diamonds.

Length

Determining if a selection of diamonds will all fit into a channel is the final segment of a compatibility study. The most common problems having to do with the mounting and diamonds should be detected prior to this stage. Comparing an order of diamonds to the channel length is frequently done at a glance. When a close tolerance is suspected, the diamonds can be spaced on top of the channel walls to check (See Fig. 1.4). If a test is necessary, it might be helpful to first apply a thin film of bees wax on the metal and position the diamonds with the table facets down. That will keep them from slipping. In many designs, though not all, it is favorable for a channel effect to set the diamonds girdle to girdle. However, if a channel is long in comparison, then a separation between the diamonds might have to be compromised. A channel that is too short can usually be modified by machining processes without disturbing the design. Another sometimes feasible alternative to consider in either extreme, but less frequently applied, is to add or delete the number of diamonds.

INSPECTION 11

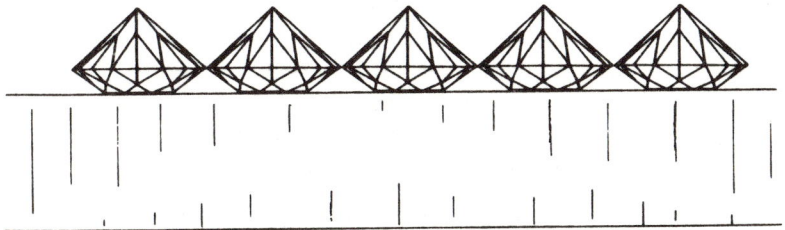

Fig. 1.4 Shows diamonds placed table facets down on a channel to compare the length requirements.

Inspecting the mounting and diamonds is vital to an organized channel setting procedure. To proceed without this knowledge could be detrimental in several aspects. It is necessary for self protection, problem perception, and craftsmanship gratification. The information collected is of the utmost importance in the layout phase when a strategy is planned for the remainder of the procedure. An experienced diamond setter will at the end of this phase already have an estimate of whether the task to come will be an agony or provide self satisfaction. Inspecting the mounting and diamonds normally only takes a few minutes, but it can save hours of frustration.

2

Layout

A layout is the development of a strategy to assemble the mounting and diamonds. For the most part, the influential characteristics of each are detected beforehand during the inspection phase. These are taken into account throughout the procedure. The task now is to determine how the selected diamonds as a group can be properly channel set into that particular mounting. A descriptive plan is necessary in order to control the procedure. Since the success of each phase is dependent upon subsequent actions, it is imperative to anticipate the effects of each move. The precise strategy will in many ways be determined by the characteristics of the mounting and diamonds.

To a diamond setter the mounting is the center of attention. Effects of machining, engraving, and other mechanical activities that it will be subjected to should be known and expected. This knowledge develops from experience working with precious metal, namely-previous diamond setting, but not necessarily channel setting. In order for the procedure to continue smoothly, a diamond setter should take time to carefully consider the effects that each move associated with the metal will have. Provisions, of course, are that the mounting and diamonds are compatible. A number of things are done to prepare a mounting for the layout and ultimately channel setting diamonds into it. Also, within limitations, adjustments can be made to a mounting for it to accept diamonds that do not readily fit. Minor adjustments to a channel are presented in this phase during the discussion of layout preparations. More extensive modifications are discussed in the following phase — CUT THE CHANNEL beginning on page 19.

The condition of the diamonds is a determining factor as to where and how they should be set. If at all feasible it is best for cosmetic purposes to position diamonds where defects such as flaws will be less noticeable. Round diamonds can be turned to where the metal will cover some imperfections, but many fancy cuts must be set as they are. Specific locations of diamonds according to size are usually restricted by the design of the mounting.

Another thing to consider concerning the diamonds is the cut. The slope of the pavilion, table facet height, and girdle thickness, all require attention. One basic theory of channel setting suggests that when setting a row of diamonds, the bearings are cut to a prescribed depth into each side of the channel. That statement is ambiguous. Specifically, bearings should be cut to a median level. In order for a series of diamonds to set in a uniform arrangement, they must be individually seated to a level where their table facets are in a consistant order. Not all diamonds are the same size, nor do they have the same quality of cut. Since the characteristics of diamonds vary, then the setting of each will also vary.

The layout is a crucial phase toward attaining a desirable completion to channel setting. It is emphatically recommended that the precise placement of each diamond be carefully planned. Perfection is particular to channel setting because corrections are usually more tedious and time consuming than if it were done right the first time. Poor judgments made in an early phase often have a lasting effect. Likewise, some mistakes that cannot be fully compensated result in a devastating effect on the finished product. During the layout a diamond setter should foresee and prevent problems that could develop throughout the remainder of the procedure. Consequently, a picture of the finished work will be envisioned. In general, the techniques that will be applied to each succeeding phase is thought out at this time.

A strategy to channel set diamonds assumes three developmental aspects: first, preparing the surface of the mounting; second, deciding exactly where each diamond will be set; and finally, the location of each diamond is noted on the metal. The layout is a trial-and-error process that involves temporarily positioning diamonds on the channel and marking their locations. Care and thought is essential in order to arrange the diamonds where they will be most favorably expressed. Upon completion of the layout the diamond setter should have a clear understanding as to precisely where and how each diamond will be set.

LAYOUT PREPARATIONS

A mounting that is to be channel set with diamonds usually requires some layout preparation. In order for the diamonds to be laid out uniformly and their positions noted, the surface of the mounting should be pre-finished. The task might be a brief filing or corrective shaping. Jewelry mechanics are ordinarily expected to refine castings according to the design, but final preparations are performed by the diamond setter. Some common occurrences are uneven channel walls, channels that are too wide or too narrow, and depressed surfaces that are supposed to be flat. Failure to correct any of these inadequacies will directly affect the layout phase and subsequently the completed assembly.

The most common problem having to do with the layout preparation is a mounting that has uneven or unparallel walls. Designs dictate straight sections, curvatures, and tapers. In all cases the adjacent sections should be symmetric. For example, assume that a straight row of diamonds is to be channel set, and one side of the channel has a high spot. Now imagine that a bearing is cut for a diamond according to usual procedure to an equal depth into each side of the channel. That diamond will not be set on a level plane to the others. To ensure that the channel walls are parallel, the top surface of each should be lightly filed together (See Fig. 1.5). Low and high areas will be revealed by the file marks. It is equally important to inspect the channel from an end and side view to be assured that both sides are consistent to the design.

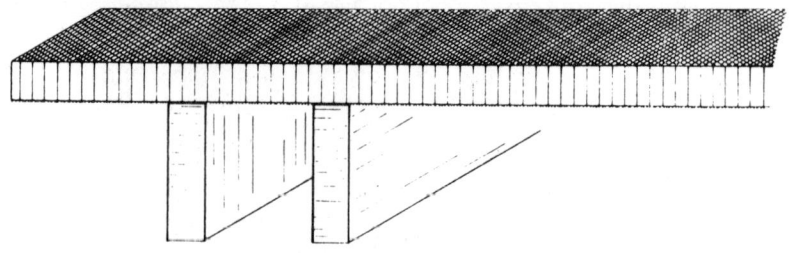

Fig. 1.5 Shows the top surface of channel walls being filed together to ensure that they are parallel.

Another typical preparation problem of a precut channel is the spacing between channel walls. This can sometimes be reasonably corrected by bending the metal in or out with appropriately shaped pliers if the walls are narrow. Adjusting the width of a channel that has wider walls is discussed on page 35. When adjusting a channel, the entire length of each wall should be moved (a little at a time) not just the individual locations where each diamond is to be set; otherwise, excessive filing will be required later to smooth the metal. The sides of the mounting are likely to become indented somewhat, but the damage can be minimized by using pliers with jaws that conform to the metal. Do not try to smooth distorted metal until the finishing phase, because other abrasions will undoubtedly occur during the procedure. If the mounting is continually resurfaced, there will be less metal available for the finishing phase. Adjusting the channel width is also a problem solving technique that may be considered during the course of channel setting.

A third task pertaining to the layout preparation is to be sure that the intended contour of the surfaces are indeed shaped that way. It is related to the problem of correcting parallel channel walls, but not all channels have walls that readily bend to secure the diamonds. Some channels are thinly cut into wide areas of metal. In those cases it is important that the entire area is first planed to eliminate distractions from the layout, and so that less metal will have to be removed during the finishing phase. Metal can be planed by filing at cross angles with a flat file until the file marks cover the surface by one draw. Cross filing is to first file in one direction, then file 45°—90° to that direction (See Fig. 1.6). Depending upon the amount of metal to be removed, a coarser file can be used to begin, but conclude with a fine cut file. Emery paper may also be considered but should not be used extensively because it will tend to round the metal. The contour of the design should not be altered; however, it should be perfected if necessary so that when the diamonds are set, they will support the design.

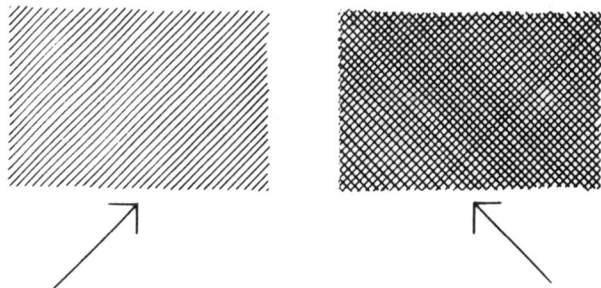

Fig. 1.6   Illustrates a 45°-90° cross filing technique to ensure that a large area of metal is plane.

Preliminary steps taken before the actual layout does not suggest that a major alteration is warranted. The purpose is for the diamond setter to be assured that the diamonds will be set according to the design. A related benefit is that layout markings to follow can be made more distinguishable. Also, because of the attractiveness of some blank mountings, especially if they are pre-polished, it is easy to overlook the imperfections; therefore, the diamond setter should personally prepare the mounting for a layout. By doing so the factors of assurance of design, clarity of layout markings, and avoidance of deception by a complex mounting will all be accounted for.

LAYOUT THE DIAMONDS

Arranging the diamonds into a logical order is the strategic aspect of a layout. Some important things to keep in mind are the specific placement of each diamond, uniformity, and equal spacing. The design will, to a certain extent, be the determining factor as to the general location where the diamonds are to be set; however, the diamond setter has limited options to control the precise placement and positioning of each. Responsibility is further increased as the variety of quality and quantity of the diamonds being set increase. Any compromise to tolerance that is given during this sub phase will be revealed in the subsequent phases of the procedure.

To begin the layout, rub a thin film of bees wax across the top of each channel wall. Bees wax will allow the diamonds to be positioned without

16 LAYOUT

shifting easily. It will smear uniformly if the mounting is first warmed slightly over an open flame. Use an extention such as pliers or tweezers to hold the mounting momentarily over the flame. By positioning the diamonds' table facets down, they will remain level. The circumferences of the girdle facets are the only dimensions of importance during this phase; therefore, trial fitting the diamonds upside down as suggested is acceptable.

Select the best uniform arrangement. Try to place the higher quality diamonds where they will be more exposed such as near the center. Likewise, if it is feasible, place the smaller and lower quality diamonds in less conspicuous areas. The design will restrict much decision making, but some creativity can usually be expressed. The options are enhanced by a variety of quality and increasing amount of diamonds. Do not be satisfied with the first layout. Different arrangements should be experimented before a final decision is made. A uniform layout is important in order for the channel walls to be symmetrically finished later in the procedure.

The spacing between channel set diamonds should be equal or proportionate to their size. Large gaps are distracting if they are not consistent. An ideal channel setting will have diamonds set girdle to girdle, but that is not always mandatory. Some designs call for separations. More often the diamonds have to be spread in order to consume the length of the channel. It is unusual though, that uneven spacing is intended. The clearance between diamonds can be arranged easily at this time. Later in the procedure it might be too late to adjust the spacing without distorting the channel walls.

Positioning diamonds on a channel setting to obtain the most effective appearance requires decision making. It is not a random process but does necessitate trial and error. At times the placement is obvious, but more often than not there are alternatives. The diamond setter has the responsibility to set the diamonds into the most attractive arrangement. With the diamonds laid out, an image of the completed work can be perceived. By having an idea of what the channel setting will look like before it is finished helps to continue the procedure smoothly. Similarly, the plan devised during this phase will directly influence the quality of the finished jewelry.

MARK THE LAYOUT

After the diamonds are laid out, and still intact on the channel by bees wax, the precise location of each is indicated by marking the metal. These engravings can be made with either a scriber or pointed graver. The purpose of the plot is to guide machining processes where each diamond is to be set without the presence of those diamonds. A diamond setter could get by with only a few tick marks to distinguish borders between diamonds on a basic

LAYOUT 17

channel mounting. For more complex designs several indications might be necessary. When the diamonds are removed, and the bees wax is rubbed off, the marks can be extended to clarify the layout. Layout marks are not fully completed with the diamonds intact because the tool could cause them to shift out of position. Depending upon the design and characteristics of the diamonds the engravings may range to extensive arcs, lines, and tick marks.

The marking requirements for the simplest channel setting might require only one or two small marks between the diamonds. If the diamonds are to be set girdle to girdle in a straight line one mark will be sufficient between the diamonds on each side of the channel (See Fig. 1.7). Two marks on each side are necessary between diamonds that are laid out with a space between them. A curved channel having diamonds laid out close together will need one mark between each diamond on the inside channel wall, and two on the outside. Since the tolerance is frequently minimal, it is a good habit to note even the smallest spaces. After the diamonds are removed from the layout, the notations will serve as reference points until the diamonds are seated.

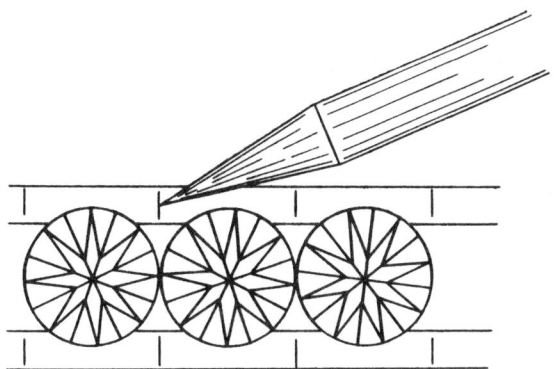

Fig. 1.7 Shows layout markings on a pre-cut channel.

Some channel settings necessitate elaborate layout engravings. Assume, for example, that the channel is not pre-cut. If the diamond setter has to cut a channel setting into a solid plate, the layout phase is more involved (See Fig. 1.8). Tick marks are engraved between each diamond as usual but also at the edges to denote the outer limits. Then the diamonds are removed and border lines are extended across the plate with a scriber and along the edges by a compass (See Fig. 1.8(B)). The centers for drilling are located by diagonal lines. All of these layout markings are made to represent diamonds in their absence and their centers. The complete method to cut a channel will be discussed later. For now it is worthy to mention that the necessary markings for various channel settings will differ.

18 LAYOUT

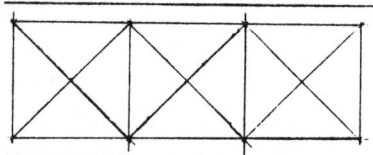
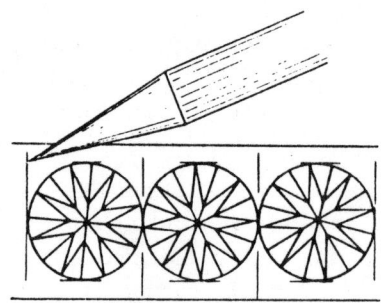

Fig. 1.8 (A) Shows layout-tick marks engraved by a scriber alongside diamonds on a solid plate.

(B) Shows the layout extended and diagonal lines made to locate centers for drilling.

There is no standard sequence to mark the layout locations of diamonds. For some experienced diamond setters a minimum number of marks are suitable in most cases. The extent of the markings is not as important as the accuracy to which they are made. Later when the bearings are cut according to the reference points, any mistakes made during this phase will evolve and interrupt that technique. To avoid the unnecessary burden of re-cutting, and possibly un-repairable conditions, precision marking is essential. Investing a little time to ensure accuracy in the layout will ultimately benefit the entire channel setting procedure.

Upon completion of the layout phase, a mental image of the finished assembly should be apparent. With the aid of a layout, a plan is devised to follow throughout each phase of the procedure. That plan, or strategy, is the foundation from where all subsequent phases develop and progress. It is imperative that the layout includes detailed markings that denote precise locations for each diamond. Without this reference the placement of diamonds would tend to be at random. Random distribution is self defeating to the cause. In order to obtain the most attractive arrangement of diamonds, a plan is of the utmost importance.

3

Cut The Channel

Since the location of a channel is predetermined by the jewelry design, the dimensions are cut to a shape that conforms to that design. The following discussion describes how to cut a channel into a solid plate. It is a frequent requirement, although most channel settings are pre-cut. A more practical reason for acquiring the information is that even pre-cut channels often require a certain amount of modification. Holes are not always properly cast, and the dimensions of a channel are not always suitable for the selected diamonds. In either situation a diamond setter should have the knowledge of how a channel setting is made. The information will occasionally be useful in its entirety but more often for improving an existing channel.

DRILL THE HOLES

One prerequisite to making a channel after the layout is to drill holes. Drilling, an eventual necessity in this case, is preferably done before other machining; otherwise, accurate spacing and centering judgments would be cumbersome. Properly aligned holes serve as permanent reference points from where all other machining evolves. The placement of each hole is regulated by the layout marks that were previously engraved on the metal. Another restriction, besides boundary limits, is that drilling should be done perpendicular to the contour of the metal (See Fig. 1.9). This is an acquired skill that results in uniformly spaced openings underneath the plate. Crossing and drilling off center, or through the side of the plate, is a mark of shoddy workmanship.

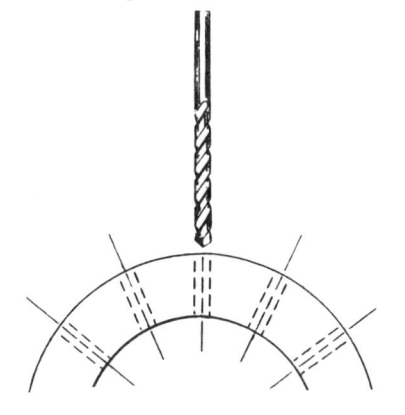

Fig. 1.9 Shows holes drilled perpendicular to the contour of a solid mounting at each location.

20 CUT THE CHANNEL

The diameter of the holes depends upon the sizes of the mounting and diamonds. Large holes, in comparison to the mounting, represent an unnecessary amount of work, and offer little room for adjustments if they are drilled off course. Very tiny holes are less functional and consequently require a drill that can easily break. An average diameter hole can be attained with an approximate NO. 60-65 size drill. A drill this size can be used for most channel setting. The hole can be enlarged later if desired. The purpose of holes is to guide boring and bearing cutting activities and to allow the finished jewelry to be cleaned; therefore, they do not have to be very large, but they should not be too small either.

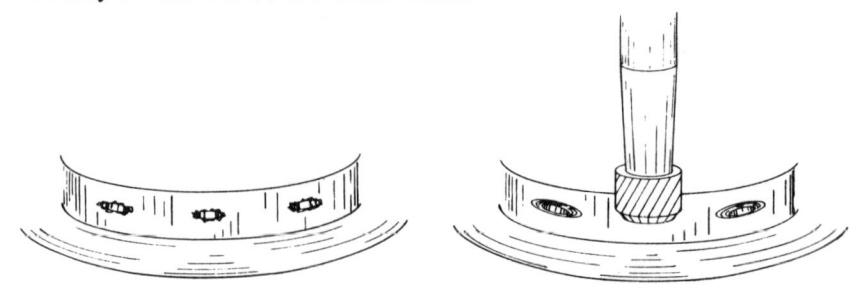

Fig. 1.10 Shows metal burrs extending from drill openings under a solid band being smoothed by an oversize setting bur.

After the holes are drilled, metal burrs usually extend from the openings. This happens when the drill completes a hole underneath the plate. The problem is that the burrs can cause a discomfort to the wearer of the jewelry, and the holes are unsightly. To remove the burrs and smooth the metal, use an oversized setting bur, or similar type, to counter-taper bore the holes (See Fig. 1.10). Also, the holes might have to be adjusted to appear centered and equally spaced by "pulling the holes." A small bud bur is suitable to do this. It is done by inserting the bur into a hole and counter boring the opening in a direction that is uniform to the spacing of the other holes. Whether or not any holes are pulled, they should all have the same diameter bore at the openings.

TAPER BORE THE HOLES

Holes are taper bored for two reasons. First, to excavate the bulk of excess metal to facilitate bearing and channel cutting that require more precision. This is a matter of enlarging the holes to a shape that will roughly conform to the diamonds while leaving a narrow opening underneath. By being relieved of that task, the cutting burs and gravers can operate with increased precision. The second reason for taper boring metal has to do with the layout. It is evident by looking at the layout that there are boundaries with minimum tolerances to adhere to. The burs selected for taper boring can vary among

CUT THE CHANNEL 21

bud burs, flame burs, and the like. These types of burs are easily maneuverable. They can enlarge holes as specified, and they can make adjustments pertaining to the layout boundary restrictions.

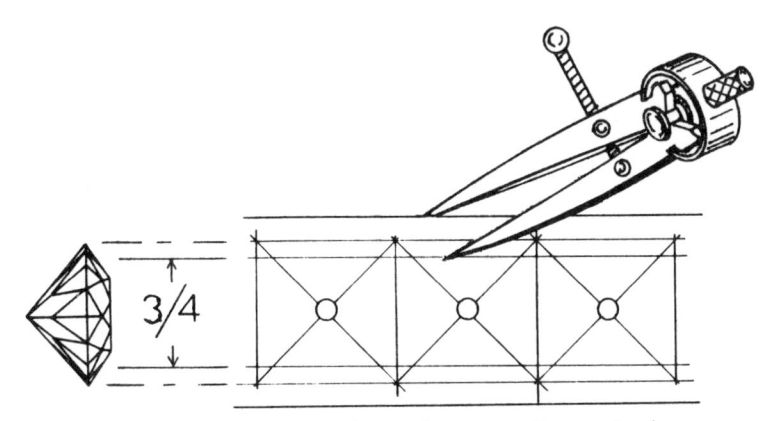

Fig. 1.11 Shows dividers being used to engrave lines centered on a plate to serve as boundaries for taper boring and reaming holes.

To taper bore holes into a solid plate, first use dividers to engrave two additional lines onto the top of the plate that are equally distant from each edge. (See Fig. 1.11). Furthermore, the distance between the two lines should be about three-fourths the diameter of the diamonds. These two lines and other layout markings will serve to center taper boring and later as boundaries for counter reaming the holes.

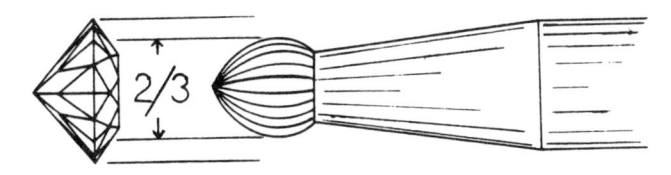

Fig. 1.12 Illustrates an appropriate size bud bur for taper boring holes.

Use a taper-bore cutting bur that is about two-thirds diameter of the diamonds (See Fig. 1.12, 1.13., and 1.14). Taper bore one hole centered between the two lines to a depth where the widest part of the bur is estimated to be at the proposed basin level. The exact depth of a basin, if there is to be one, has no standard, but there is one stipulation: for a channel effect it should be cut below the depth where the girdles of the diamonds will ultimately be seated. A bearing is cut to a depth that is one and one half times the distance between the girdle of a diamond to its table facet. At that depth the table facet will set favorably just below the top of the channel; therefore, the basin should be cut below that depth. If all the diamonds are the same size, then the taper bores should be equal.

22 CUT THE CHANNEL

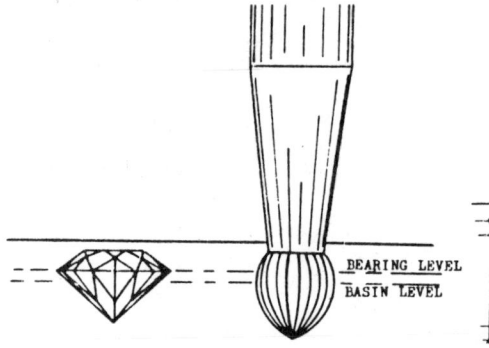

Fig. 1.13 Shows the depth to taper bore a hole for channel cutting.

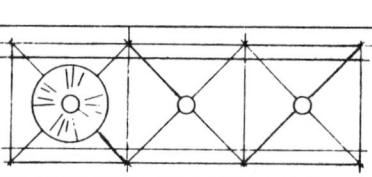

Fig. 1.14 Shows the completion of a taper bore centered between the boundary lines.

Adjust dividers from the outside edge of the channel to the nearest edge of the first bore (See Fig. 1.15). The adjustment should be likewise from both sides. Then extend the lines along the channel to serve as diameter borders for other taper bores to keep them in line. Taper bore the holes a little at a time, making adjustments along the way, until each one is at the appropriate width, depth, spacing, and centered between the border lines.

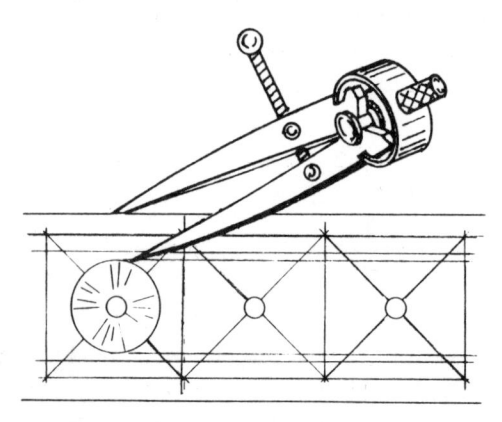

Fig. 1.15 Illustrates dividers extending lines from the edges of the first taper bore to serve as a guide to cut the others in line.

COUNTER REAM THE HOLES

After excavating excessive metal from the holes, additional metal is extruded in a more precise manner by reaming. Counter reaming is done as an outlining measure to distinguish the width and depth of the channel. A setting bur is used because of its combination cylindrical/taper shape. It can cut a straight bore that results in a consistent width. Also, its vertex (the point where the cylinder and taper meet) creates a distinctive ridge in the metal that is used as a guide to cut the basin. An additional benefit of a setting bur is that its lower portion cuts a taper into the basin that conforms to the pavilion of the diamonds.

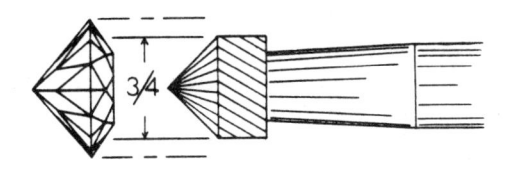

Fig. 1.16 Shows the appropriate size setting bur to ream holes.

Use a setting bur having a size that is three-fourths the diameter of the diamonds (See Fig. 1.16). The channel will later be cut to the width of the resulting cylindrical cuts. Counter ream each hole keeping the bur centered and adjoining the two border lines. And cut to a depth where the vertex of the bur reaches the proposed basin level (See Fig. 1.17). A channel cut at three-fourths the diameter of the diamonds will have an effective "channel appearance." At the same time the diamond will extend sufficiently enough from each side of the channel to be secured by both channel walls.

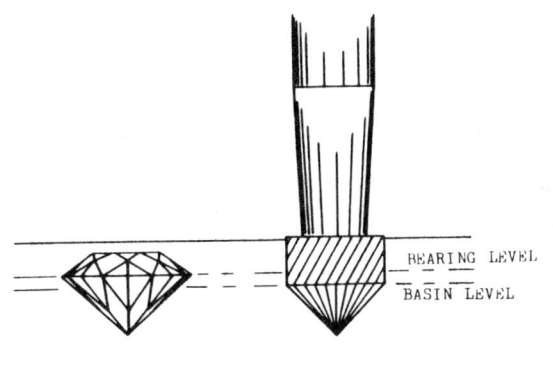

Fig. 1.17 Illustrates a setting bur reaming holes to the depth of a channel basin.

CUT THE CHANNEL

The method used to cut a channel depends in part upon the design and amount of metal that has to be removed. Other related variables are personal preference, skills, and available tools. Pre-cut channels normally require only a minor adjustment. Bending a wall in or out and lightly filing the top of the channel walls was discussed as a preparation for the layout. Further adjustments are not always necessary. When a pre-cut channel does not exist, such as in the solid bar being discussed, there is obviously more work

24 CUT THE CHANNEL

involved. The latter case is an extreme example. Up to this stage the diamonds have been laid out and their positions marked. Holes have been drilled, taper bored, and counter reamed. Now the channel is cut to appropriate dimensions using the reamed holes as a guide.

By applying a channel cutting technique that requires reamed holes, much of the channel becomes pre-cut. The next step is to remove the metal between them. First use a piercing saw or knife graver, whichever is applicable, to cut lengthwise barely within the edges of the reams straight down to their vertexes (See Fig. 1.18[A]). There should be two cuts — one on each side of the channel. It is important that they are made within the limits of the reamed holes to avoid cutting the channel too wide or too deep. Consideration is also given to the length. The exact dimensions can be more precisely trimmed after the bulk of metal has been removed.

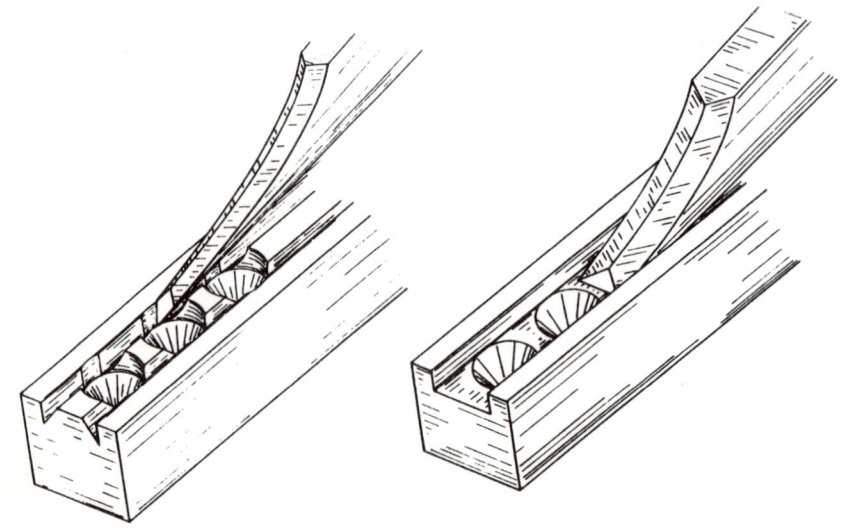

Fig. 1.18 (A) Shows a knife graver cutting within the edges of reamed holes to guide channel cutting. (B) Using a flat graver to excavate a channel to the basin.

After the dimensions are outlined by the parallel cuts, the channel is further excavated. This can be done by a variety of tools including a flat graver, square needle file, or wheel bur (See Fig. 1.18[B]). If the initial two cuts were made within the dimension limits, the metal can be rough cut. Again, stay within the guidelines of the layout markings and reams. Final trimming to the borders should be made with a flat graver or other hand operated tool in order to make precise judgments.

The completed channel should be flat at the basin and have walls that are perpendicular to it. These are important features that are helpful to estimate the correct bearing depth, thereby permitting the diamonds to be seated level. And, it is necessary to obtain an ideal channel design. Before going on with the procedure, the channel should be smoothed by a rubber wheel and pre-polished. It will be tedious to remove abrasions from inside the channel, as well as can be done now, after the diamonds are secured into it. A final check of the channel for correct dimensions is made by placing each diamond on top of the channel at the location where it will be set. From there a visual inspection can determine if the width is suitable. Also, the depth and the presence of obstructing metal can be foreseen by mentally projecting an image of the seating arrangement.

4

Cut The Bearing

The bearing for a channel set diamond is an obtuse angle (more than 90° but less than 180°) cut into the channel at opposite sides. Its purpose is to contain the girdle of the diamond and to brace the upper pavilion facets. Three important features of a bearing are the width, depth, and level. If the diameter is cut too large the diamond will be loosely seated and cause problems to develop later. Second, the bearing should be low enough that an adequate amount of metal remains above the girdle to secure the diamond. And third, it should be cut to an equal depth into each side of the channel so the diamond will set level. A bearing is useful only to the extent that all its prescribed dimensions conform to the diamond.

Bearings should be cut to respectively differ in width as diamonds differ in size. A group of diamonds selected for setting are seldom all the exact same size. Their carat weight may be labeled identical, but the actual weight is traditionally approximated to the nearest whole number and fraction in very small melee. To properly cut a bearing, the craftsman cannot likewise select the nearest size bur if it is larger than the diamond. Diamonds should be seated tight in their bearings. Otherwise, they could tilt out of level when attempting to secure them or eventually become loose. Also, because of a gap created between the girdle of a diamond that is seated loose and the channel wall, the finish is likely to become distorted. Channel setting diamonds is tedious enough without having the burden of correcting an oversized bearing. In order for the procedure to continue along an organized pattern, the diamonds have to fit snugly into the bearings prior to actually securing them; therefore, the width of each bearing is cut just enough to contain the diamond being set there.

The bearing depth in a channel setting is the distance between the top of the channel walls and the vertex of the bearing. A vertex is the point from where the bearing angle changes. When a diamond is seated, its girdle should adjoin the vertex. Metal that extends above the girdle is later formed onto the diamond to secure it. If a bearing is cut too deep, the depth and level could be misinterpreted, especially in comparison to adjacent bearings. Also, there will be an excessive amount of metal to finish after the diamond is secured. Cutting a bearing too shallow will result in the diamond seated high. In that case the metal above the diamond might be such a small amount that it will be reluctant to bend, or there might not be enough to sufficiently secure the diamond and obtain an attractive finish. An ideal bearing depth for a channel set diamond is where the diamond can be seated with its table facet slightly lower than the top of the channel.

Diamonds are notable set level between each side of the channel and conform to adjacent diamonds. The intention is to have the table facets of all diamonds on a fixed plane following the contour of the channel. Cutting the bearings level is a matter of control and perspective abilities of the diamond setter. Some compromise is necessary when one or more diamonds have unequal cut crown facets causing the table to be slanted. Specifically, this will occur when rose cut and old mine cut diamonds are being set. The result of a bearing that is not level is usually a distractive and possibly unsecure diamond.

The dimensions of a bearing will invariably have an effect on the finished setting. When a diamond is seated too low, more work is involved to expose it. Conversely, if a diamond is seated too high, there might not be enough metal to finish or to secure the diamond. Finally, the diamond must be set level in order for it to be presented to its fullest advantage. The specifications for a channel bearing offers very little tolerance. Only the prescribed dimensions comply with other phases of the procedure.

BEARING CUTTING TOOLS AND TECHNIQUES

Several different tools and techniques can be used to cut the bearings for channel set diamonds. The decision depends upon numerous factors. Among them is the fact that particular shapes of diamonds and types of channels restrict the use of certain tools. For instance, burs can be used to cut bearings for round diamonds, but gravers are preferred to carve bearings to contain the girdles of square cut diamonds and the like. Also, channels differ in that one type might be *open* with a vacant area extending well below the diamonds. Another type of channel is *closed* by a basin at the pavilion level. Generally, the method to cut the bearings into a channel depends upon the shape of the diamond being set and the type of channel. The final decision is determined by the diamond setter with consideration towards experience and personal preference. Whatever technique is applied to ensure a good seat for the diamond is of little consequence provided the bearing's dimensional prerequisites are met.

A variety of tools are applicable to cut bearings into a channel setting. One of the most popular is a hart bur. It has an undercutting capability and a shallow pavilion angle that provides access into the channel if the bur is tilted. Some other bearing cutting burs can be troublesome if undercutting

28 CUT THE BEARING

is required. When a bur is tilted into a channel to undercut a bearing, its lower portion must not be restricted from entering the channel. Either the opposite channel wall or an existing basin in the channel will prohibit the use of certain types of burs. If a diamond setter chooses not to undercut, then a high speed setting bur can be used to vertical cut the bearings. Another alternative is to use a knife and flat graver. These are especially useful to cut bearings for diamonds that have straight girdles such as square, baguette, and emerald cut diamonds. One disadvantage of hand gravers is that their use requires more effort than machine tools unless a machine such as a Gravermeister or GraverMax is available (See Fig. 1.19). Several tools, both hand and machine, can be used in conjunction to cut a single bearing.

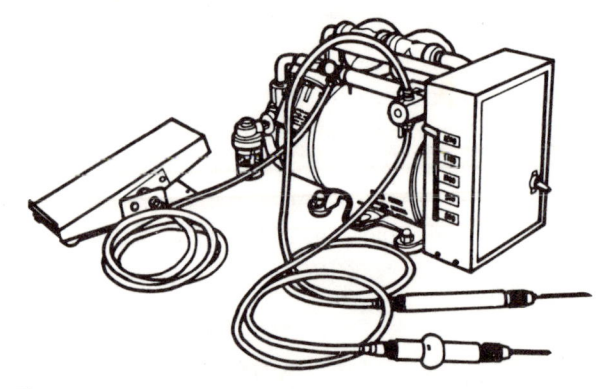

Fig. 1.19 Gravermeister by GRS Engraving Products. A machine tool that provides controlled power to gravers.

Cutting bearings with gravers is at times a necessity, especially when channel setting fancy cut diamonds. Gravers are capable of making straight cuts that conform to the girdle facets of those diamonds, whereas the use of burs is limited. Frequently, some burs are useful to remove excessive metal prior to the use of gravers. All diamonds consume a certain amount of space in a channel. It is easier to remove excess metal with a machine tool whenever possible rather than using a hand operated tool. When cutting bearings for diamonds that have straight girdles, burs are often used in the process, but gravers offer more precision to complete the bearings.

VERTICAL CUT BEARINGS

A vertical cut bearing is typically cut into channels. Basically it is similar to many other diamond setting bearings. A vertical cut is made into the channel walls to a predetermined depth. At that point a vertex is created by the lower angle that conforms to the pavilion of a diamond. The most common use for a vertical cut bearing in channels is in conjunction with an undercut bearing on the opposite channel wall. Another occasional reason is when the metal is too thin for other bearing cutting techniques. An example of that is when a diamond is being replaced in a worn mounting. Sometimes in decisive cases such as an extremely wide channel, where only the lower portion of a bearing can be cut, a vertical cut bearing is a problem solving solution. Since there are so many circumstances that influence how a vertical bearing is cut, a single technique in the matter cannot be universally recommended.

High speed setting burs are practical to cut vertical bearings into channels for round diamonds because of the bur's upper cylindrical shape and the lower taper that extends from it. They can cut straight down into the metal, leaving an equal perpendicular rise on both sides of the channel and a bearing that conforms to the diamond (See Fig. 1.20). Setting burs can also be used in part to pre-excavate metal to fit straight faceted diamonds, particularly square cuts. In that case gravers would be used to trim the metal afterwards. Under certain conditions vertical bearings for both round and fancy cut diamonds may be cut with gravers.

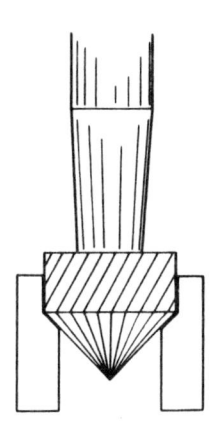

Fig. 1.20 Illustrates a setting bur cutting a vertical bearing into a channel.

Using gravers to cut vertical bearings into a channel allows alternate techniques. For frequent situations they are indispensible. There are several shapes, sizes, and combinations of gravers that can be used. A flat graver alone is versatile enough to cut vertical bearings for ordinary channels. To cut the bearing's vertical rise, position the flat graver as shown in figure 1.21. With the cutting edge at the bearing depth, make long shaving strokes. The bearing's lower angle is formed by cutting with the graver slanted downward (See Fig. 1.22). Switch between both positions to inspect and adjust the width and depth. Neither this technique nor any other can be labeled as to how all vertical bearings should be cut. It is merely an elective among the vast resources available.

30 CUT THE BEARING

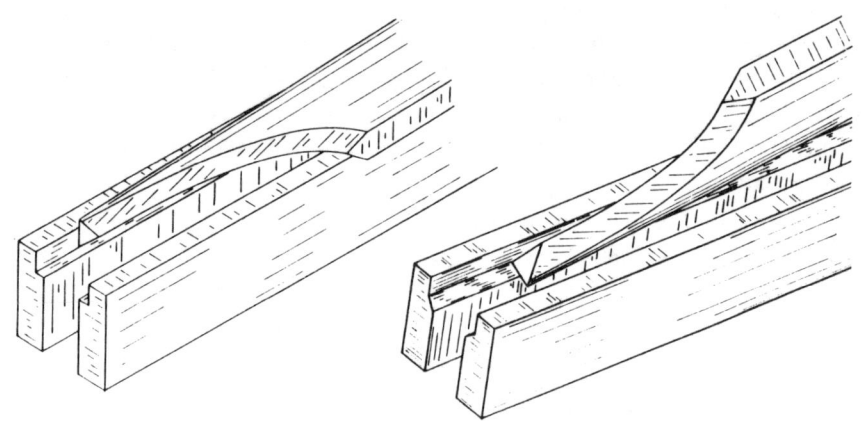

Fig. 1.21 Shows a flat graver cutting the vertical rise for a channel bearing.

Fig. 1.22 Shows a flat graver positioned at a lower slant to cut the pavilion angle of a bearing in a channel.

The best technique concerning the appropriate tool to vertical cut a bearing depends upon the task at hand. Burs and gravers each have advantages over the other, but there are also disadvantages. One drawback to using a setting bur is that it cuts inlets into the channel walls. Small inlets are desirable because they contain the diamonds. Larger inlets result in excessive metal between the diamonds. If some of the metal between large inlets is not removed before securing the diamonds, it will cause finishing problems. Using a graver to vertical cut bearings is often necessary, but a continuous bearing on each side of the channel could allow the diamonds to slide. Unless the diamonds are seated into a basin or girdle to girdle, extra care will have to be taken to maintain equal spacing.

UNDERCUTTING

Undercutting is a commonly applied option to cut bearings into a channel. The result is a ledge that contains a diamond while the metal from the opposite side is worked to secure it. Stabilizing diamonds is particularly important when hammer setting to secure them into a channel. Only one wall is undercut, otherwise the diamond will not slip snugly into the bearings. It may be cut by either a hart bur or gravers A hart bur is ideal to undercut bearings for round diamonds because of its shape. Gravers can also be used to undercut bearings for round diamonds, but are better suited for straight faceted diamonds. Both techniques are discussed independently in the following two segments.

Undercutting Bearings For Round Diamonds

Using a hart bur to undercut a bearing into a channel is a skill by itself. One wall is undercut while the opposite wall is simultaneously vertical cut. Before applying power, tilt the bur into the channel towards the side that is to be undercut. Center it between border markings with the cutting edge at the proposed bearing level, and position the shaft at a vertical axis to the channel (See Fig. 1.23). First make a small test cut to be sure that the beginning of the bearing is at the right depth and level. At first a certain amount of effort will be needed to control the bur. If the bearing is satisfactory so far, then undercutting may begin with the bur held in that position.

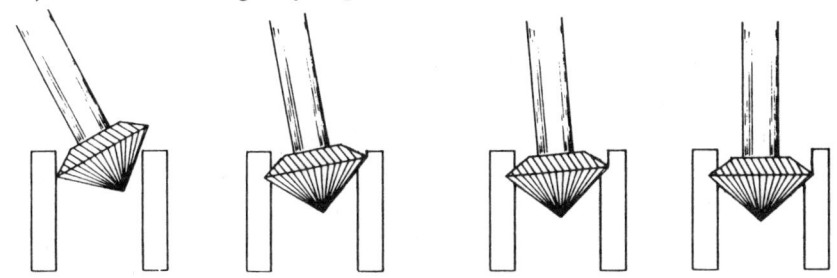

Fig. 1.23 Illustrates an undercutting technique using a hart bur.

Undercutting one side of a channel and vertical cutting the opposite side at the same time should be done in one continuous operation. Otherwise, the bearings could become ridged. To do this position the hart bur into the channel as before, then slowly graduate the power until the bur begins to cut comfortably under control. Continue to cut proportionately less into the undercut while tilting the bur shaft back to make a vertical cut down the opposite wall (See Fig. 1.23). The power usually has to be increased to medium speeds at this point. Stop when the bur shaft is nearly perpendicular to the channel. Sometimes a rise develops in the undercut that allows the diamond to be seated level. If the diamond will not seat level, then re-insert the hart bur under power and bring the shaft to a full perpendicular position.

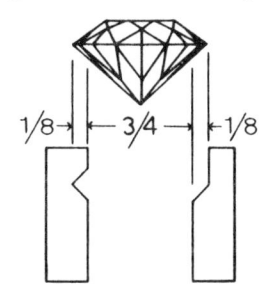

Fig. 1.24 Shows the bearing dimensions cut into each channel wall.

32 CUT THE BEARING

Upon completion the same distance should be cut into each channel wall, although one wall is undercut and one vertical cut to the bearing. In other words, if the channel is three-fourths the diameter of the diamond, then there will be one-fourth remaining. Therefore, the lateral distance cut into each wall should be about one-eighth the diameter of the diamond (See Fig. 1.24). To seat the diamond, tilt it into the undercut wall then push down on the opposite side.

Undercutting Bearings For Fancy Cut Diamonds

A channel bearing for square, baguette, or emerald cut diamonds is continuous on each side of the channel. It can be cut with either an anglette or knife graver, or a flat graver. One preferred technique is to first rough cut the metal with either graver, then refine the rough cuts with a flat graver. To make an undercut bearing on one side of the channel, hold the graver to an upward slant beginning at the proposed bearing depth (See Fig. 1.25). The slant should conform to the angle that the crown facets extend from the girdles of the diamonds. If the depth of the bearing is adequate, the top surface of the channel wall will remain uncut. The bearing depth and undercut should be consistent. An upper bearing is also cut into the opposite channel wall, but it is cut vertically from the bearing depth rather than to an angle. Then the pavilion angle is cut on both sides (See Fig. 1.26). To control the dimensions of the bearing, shave the metal a little at a time and continually inspect the results.

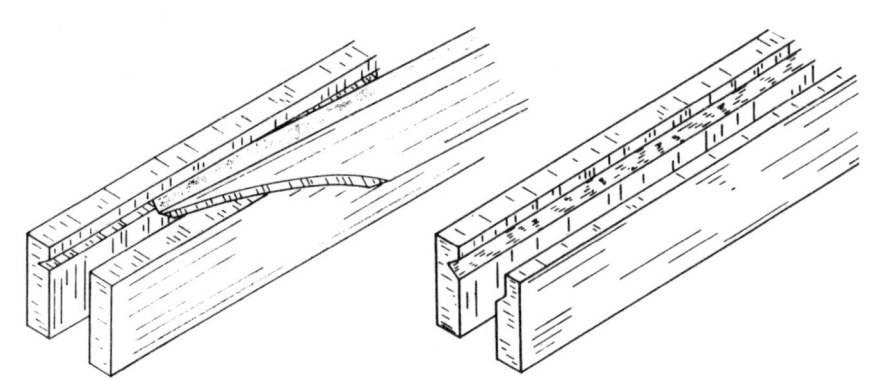

Fig. 1.25 Using a flat graver positioned at an upward slant to undercut one channel wall.

Fig. 1.26 Shows the pavilion angles cut into channel walls.

The bearing for an open channel would be completed by the preceding discussion, but a channel setting having a basin requires further preparation. A bud bur and setting bur could be used to shape a basin to contain the

CUT THE BEARING

pavilion of a round diamond but would only be a start to that for a fancy cut diamond. In order for the pavilion facets of a square or similar cut diamond to seat into the basin, the metal should also be cut with gravers. The first cuts are made with a knife or anglette graver into the basin (See Fig. 1.27). For a square cut diamond there will be four cuts squared to a common center point (or the original drilled hole). The distance between these cuts will have to be estimated by comparison to the size of each diamond being set. To complete the pavilion shaping, a flat graver is used to plane the metal between the knife graver cuts (See Fig. 1.28).

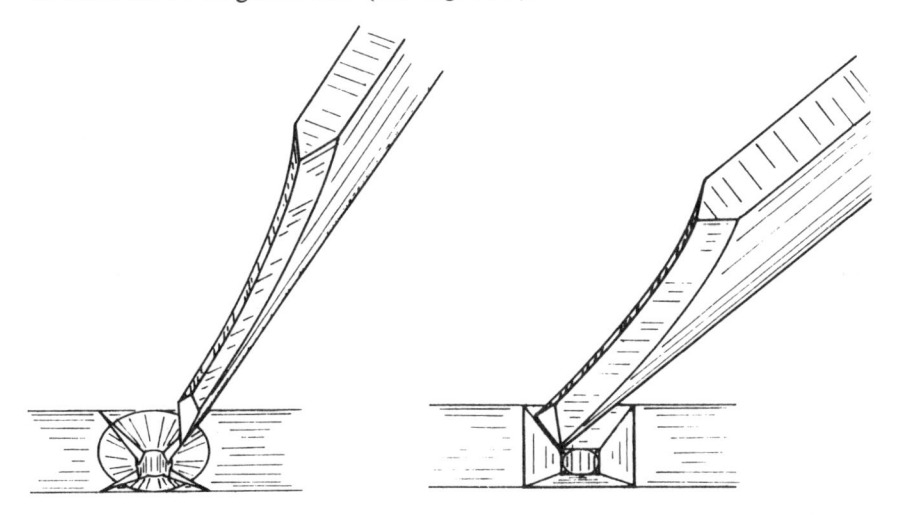

Fig. 1.27 Shows a knife graver making four squared cuts from the channel basin level down toward the holes.

Fig. 1.28 Shows a flat graver planing the channel basin metal between the knife cuts.

Adjustments will likely have to be made as each diamond is trial fitted to enlarge or recut a particular portion of the bearing. It is helpful to first try seating the diamond for each bearing table facet down. In this way the metal above the bearing can be assured of having the proper dimensions. Once it is determined that the upper section is right, then work can progress on the metal below the vertex (or bearing depth). The advantage of proceeding in this manner is that if a diamond does not fit, it will be known that the problem is in the pavilion section of the bearing, and over-cutting the upper section will be avoided.

SEAT THE DIAMONDS

Seating diamonds is the phase of channel setting when diamonds are fitted into the channel. Afterwards they will finally be secured. The step is

34 CUT THE BEARING

interrelated with cutting bearings, but distinct in that it immediately precedes securing the diamonds. Adjustments are often necessary in order to correct inadequacies that have occurred up to this point in the procedure. Diamonds are expected to eventually fit according to the plan that was initiated in the layout phase. If all goes well they are then individually pre-tightened into assigned positions in order to remain stable while they are being secured. In other respects this is an opportune time to make changes in the procedure, if necessary, to avoid encountering future problems.

Seating Recommendations

To handle the diamonds, touch the table facets with a small piece of bees wax tapered to a point. When placing a diamond into position, it will have a tendency to stick to the wax. To overcome this, tilt the diamond into one side of the bearing then twist the wax to roll it off of the diamond. There should be an escape for the wax provided by the inability of the diamond to lift out from one side of the channel. The diamond can then be pressed into position by a soft but rigid material such as a fingernail or piece of wood. Also, be sure that the bearings and diamonds are clean before attempting to seat them permanently. Any debris such as wax, filings, or dirt could have an effect on proper seating.

When seating diamonds, it is especially important that they are seated tight but still removable. A snug fit will increase the possibilities that the diamonds will remain in position while they are being secured. Pressure resulting from hammering or burnishing on either side of a channel is likely to cause a loosely seated diamond to shift. On the contrary, being able to take the diamond out of the bearing without too much difficulty is beneficial in case adjustments become necessary. A diamond seated as suggested is less apt to move out of position.

Problem Solving

If a diamond will not seat as recommended because its bearing is too large, a number of corrective measures can be taken. The simplest of these is to shuffle diamonds to bearings that are more suitable. Since the bearings are previously cut, there are limitations to doing this. Another alternative is to furnish larger or smaller diamonds. Two drawbacks with that is the cost factor of furnishing larger diamonds and/or the ethics of switching diamonds. The most practical and ethical solution to solve the problem of a loosely seated diamond is done at the workbench. The workbench option is to adjust the channel walls accordingly by using pliers to pull one side slightly towards the other, or by hammering. With either of these methods only one wall should

CUT THE BEARING 35

be moved because the metal will have a tendency to expand over the channel opening. It is important to remember this when such size adjustments are performed if the bearing is undercut because the diamond is tilted into the bearing afterwards in order to seat it. If both sides are extended over the channel opening, the diamond will not be permitted to slip into the bearing.

Adjustments to the channel can be made even if the metal is too thick to move an entire wall. This is done by working the metal as if the diamonds were being secured by hammer setting (See HAMMERING/TAPPING pg. 40). With the diamonds removed use a tapping tool and chasing hammer to bend the metal from one channel wall over (See Fig. 1.29). The wall per se might not move, but the inside edge should bend over slightly. Concentrate the tapping to the inner edge of the wall. After the metal is moved over the channel, it should act as a ledge to keep the diamond from lifting out from one side. By hammering too much, the bearing might have to be recut. Once again, these are problem solving techniques to be applied only in extreme cases.

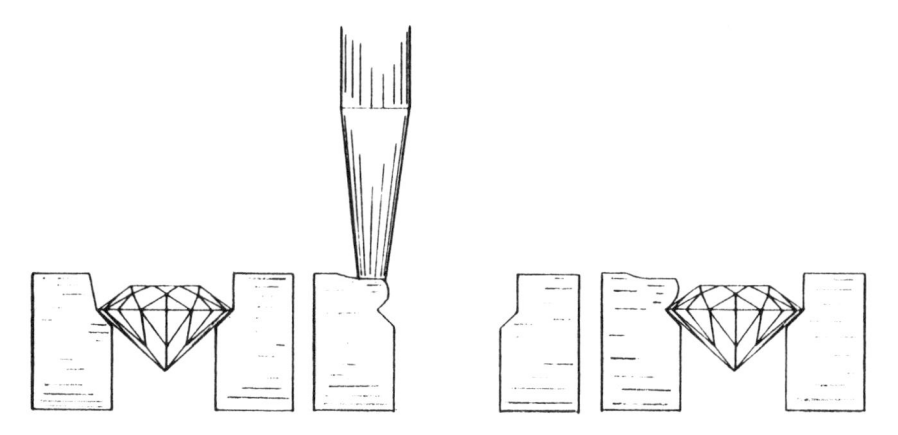

Fig. 1.29 Tapping metal to adjust wide channel walls.

After all the diamonds are seated, check to see that they are equally spaced, positioned at an adequate depth, and level. Ideally the diamonds should be seated girdle to girdle or have a slight separation. A few designs do require a distinct separation. In either case the separations between diamonds should be the same. If the diamonds are not positioned as specified in the design, corrections will have to be made accordingly. This will usually require recutting the bearing(s) for those that are out of order. When checking for proper seating, imagine the jewelry piece as being completed and critique it. Do not praise the work, but try to find things wrong with it. Once the diamonds are secured, it will be too late to change their positions or reseat them easily without altering the mounting.

36 CUT THE BEARING

The purpose of a bearing is in part to provide a stable seat for a diamond. Further considerations are given to security and finishing. To ensure the most advantageous presentation and security for the diamonds, special features of the bearing are required. These pertain to the width, depth, and level. A selection among various tools and techniques is necessary to obtain a good bearing. The decision as to what choice of techniques to apply depends upon the type of channel that is to be set, the shape of the diamonds, and the diamond setter's preference.

5

Secure The Diamonds

Three techniques are described and illustrated in this phase to secure diamonds into a channel setting. Two suggest the use of pliers, and the other is with the use of a tapping tool and chasing hammer. The application of each depends primarily upon the design of the mounting, hardness of metal, and shape of diamonds. Other variables include the diamond setter's proficiency in particular techniques. Most channel settings can be secured by applying only one technique. Conversely, it is often advantageous to combine more than one to the same channel setting. A diamond setter should have the knowledge and skills to secure diamonds into a channel by various means.

USING PLIERS TO SECURE CHANNEL SET DIAMONDS

Using the leverage advantage of pliers to exert pressure is often an appropriate means to secure channel set diamonds. Its use depends much upon the jewelry design and characteristics of the metal. The technique is commonly used for channels having metal that is capable of collapsing easily enough to bend onto the diamonds. It is not practical for wide channel walls or inlaid channels. Be aware that if too much pressure is required, because the meal is thick or stiff, pliers could cause the diamonds to chip. Also, a springing action that occurs in some cast metal could inhibit the effects of the pressure. In that case the metal would not remain in position. The technique of using pliers to secure channel set diamonds is not applicable in all situations, but when suitable it can be very effective and efficient.

The pliers used to secure diamonds into a channel should be a miniature or slimline type with innerfaced jaws that conform to the shape of the mounting. By using small pliers specific areas of the mounting can be worked independently. Any shifting of diamonds or undesirable movement of metal can be detected immediately. In contrast, larger pliers are capable of transferring too much pressure and conceal much of the work being done. All pliers cause some indention to the metal. Potential damage can be minimized by using those having compatibly shaped jaws. For instance, the flat innerface of chain nose pliers is ideal to secure straight sections. Another type such as combination-half round/flat is best for curvature shaped channels. Still,

38 SECURE THE DIAMONDS

the force produced by the pliers, whether favorable or unfavorable, depends upon the diamond setter's ability to control them.

Using Pliers To Secure Diamonds Into Vertical Cut Bearings

This is a fundamental technique involving pliers to secure diamonds into a channel. The pliers are positioned perpendicular over the diamonds with the jaws grasping opposite sides of the channel equally (See Fig. 1.30[A]). Only the outer top edges of the channel are in contact with the pliers. In that position the pressure can be evenly distributed to both sides of the channel (See Fig. 1.30[B]). A clear view is necessary to observe the diamonds as the metal bends to secure them. If a diamond begins to shift the problem can be corrected by altering the position of the jaws to apply more pressure to one side. A great deal of control is required to use this technique, but once the skill is obtained it can be applied to many channel setting situations.

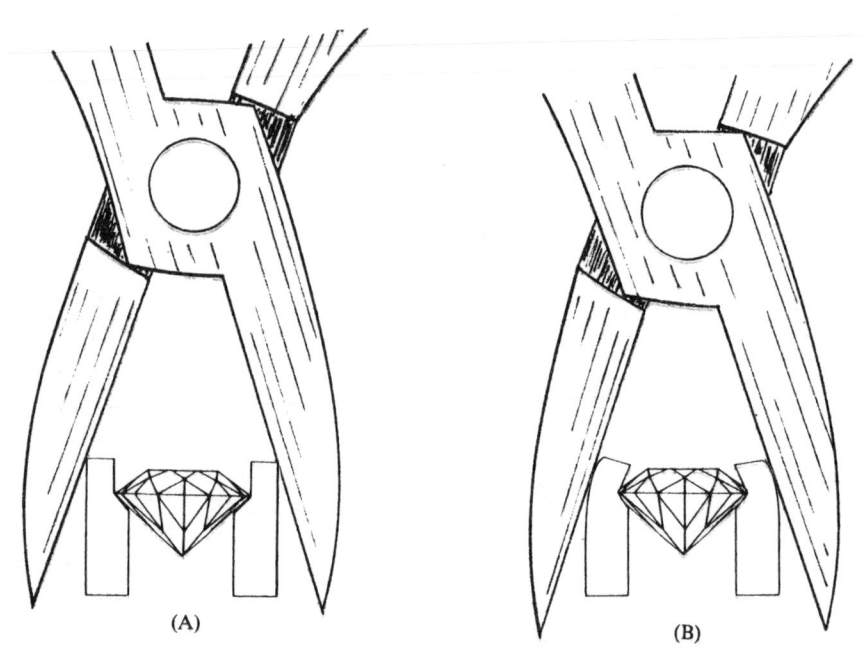

Fig. 1.30 Shows a technique using pliers to secure a diamond into a vertical cut-channel bearing.

Using Pliers To Secure Diamonds Into Undercut Bearings

The position of the pliers is the key to securing diamonds that are seated into an undercut channel. The side that is not undercut is bent onto the diamonds first; otherwise, pressure on the undercut side could cause the diamonds to lift out of the channel. Brace one jaw of the pliers flatly and

SECURE THE DIAMONDS

upright against the outside of the metal that is undercut (See Fig. 1.31[A]). This will help to keep the diamonds stable and prevent the mounting from bending at the shank. Place the other jaw against the top outside of the opposite channel wall. The angular spread of the pliers should induce them to be positioned correctly.

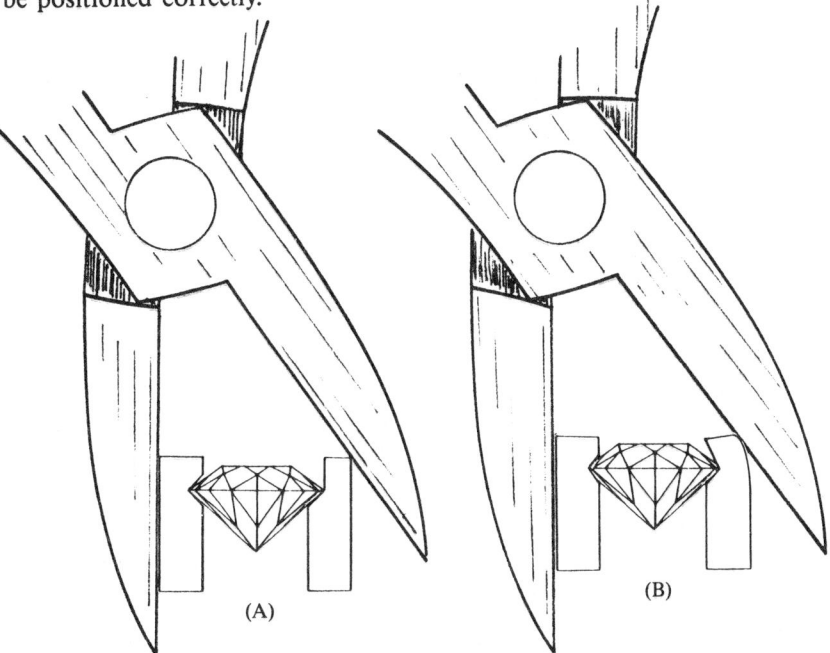

Fig. 1.31 Shows a technique using pliers to secure a diamond into an undercut — channel bearing.

To secure the diamonds, squeeze the pliers. With the undercut wall acting as a brace only the opposite wall should bend (See Fig. 1.31[B]). Slide the pliers along the channel bending the metal slightly at each diamond. Do not try to tighten the diamonds at the first pass. After the metal at each diamond is bent over just enough to keep them from lifting out, then bend the metal between the diamonds likewise. This will make the channel wall straight again. Repeat the process until all diamonds are secure and the channel wall is straight along the diamonds. With each move check to see that the diamonds have not shifted. Afterwards, repeat the technique to the undercut side of the channel by bracing the pliers against the side that was just secured. Do not apply as much pressure because the diamonds could already be tight. The purpose is to make sure that the diamonds are well fitted into the undercut.

After using pliers to secure channel set diamonds, the diamonds should be secure at the girdles; however, a gap usually exists between the crown facets and the upper portion of metal on each side of the channel. Most of this metal will be removed during the finishing phase. Gaps can be closed, at least partially, if it is desirable for extra security or cosmetic reasons. It is not advisable to use pliers to press the metal down unless it is absolutely necessary. This is done by bracing one jaw of the pliers under the channel and the other jaw on top of the channel. That will severely distort the metal underneath. The recommended method is to use a tapping tool and chasing hammer to close the gap. As stated earlier, it is possible in many situations to apply either or all of these techniques in conjunction to the same channel setting.

HAMMERING/TAPPING TO SECURE CHANNEL SET DIAMONDS

Hammering the metal to secure channel set diamonds is a handy technique to use when the metal will not readily bend. A good example of this is to secure diamonds into an inlaid channel (a channel that is centered within a large area of metal). The term "hammering" is vague because it implies an excessive force. Actually the tools used to perform the technique are lightweight. They include a tapping tool, chasing hammer, and a fixture to hold the mounting. An automatic hammer could be used instead of a chasing hammer. For discussion purposes a chasing hammer is more basic. The tools are not heavy duty but do require exceptional skill and control because of the nature of the craft.

Tapping Tool

A typical tapping tool is a rod about one-eighth inch diameter that is tapered to a flat circular tip. To ensure an even distribution of metal the tip should, within reason, be about one millimeter wide. These features will allow an unobstructed view of the metal and diamonds as the tool is being used. The length requirement is about two inches. That will allow the fingers to hold it without obstructing the view, and the end can be tapped within peripheral vision. Additionally, the tapping tool should be made from a high carbon steel, so it can be heat treated easily. Annealing is necessary in order to occasionally reshape the tip. The tip is quench hardened before being used, otherwise it will become rounded and uncontrollable. Some brands of beading tools are excellent for conversion to tapping tools simply by filing the tip flat.

SECURE THE DIAMONDS 41

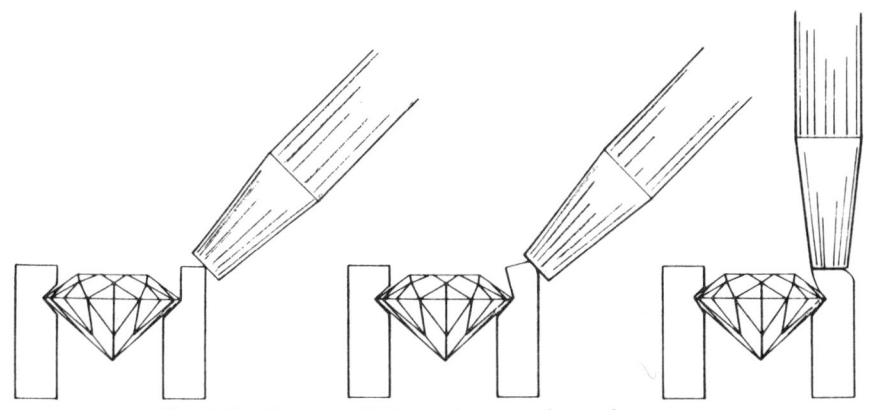

Fig. 1.32 Shows a technique using a tapping tool to secure a diamond into an undercut-channel bearing.

A tapping tool should always be held sturdy and, with few exceptions, positioned within a perpendicular axis to the channel. The exact position along the plane depends upon the direction that the metal is to move. For instance, when at first tapping the top of a narrow channel wall onto a diamond, the tool is positioned toward the crown facets of the diamond (See Fig. 1.32). Later to close a gap between the metal and the diamond, the tapping tool is placed perpendicular to the top of the channel. Do not hold the tool in a direction that will force the metal away from the diamonds. Likewise, the tool should not, in most cases, tilt to either side. A side force is likely to cause an uneven indentation in the metal because the tip will not strike flatly. A side force could also cause the jewelry piece to slip in its fixture. One exception to this rule is when a mandrel is used to channel set a ring that has a channel along the finger line. In that case slightly tilting the tapping tool towards the wide end of the mandrel will help to keep the ring from slipping. A final note is that the tip should be in constant contact with the metal in order to maintain control at all times. Similarly, to avoid serious indentation to the metal, slide the tapping tool momentarily along the channel after each time it is struck by the chasing hammer.

Chasing Hammer

The chasing hammer recommended for channel setting is lightweight, balanced, and made from a fruitwood. Fruitwood, being somewhat flexible, aids a springing action when used properly. Hold the hammer at the end of the handle with the forefinger extended along the back (See Fig. 1.33). As the face of the hammer hits the tapping tool, the force is applied and controlled by the extended finger. A rhythmic speed produced by a wrist action will help to control the hammer. The forearm should remain stable at all times.

42 SECURE THE DIAMONDS

When striking the tapping tool, it is important that the end of it is hit squarely by the face of the chasing hammer. Hitting a tapping tool at a slant could have the same effect as that of not holding the tool upright. To maintain control of the tapping tool and the work being done, the chasing hammer must also be controlled.

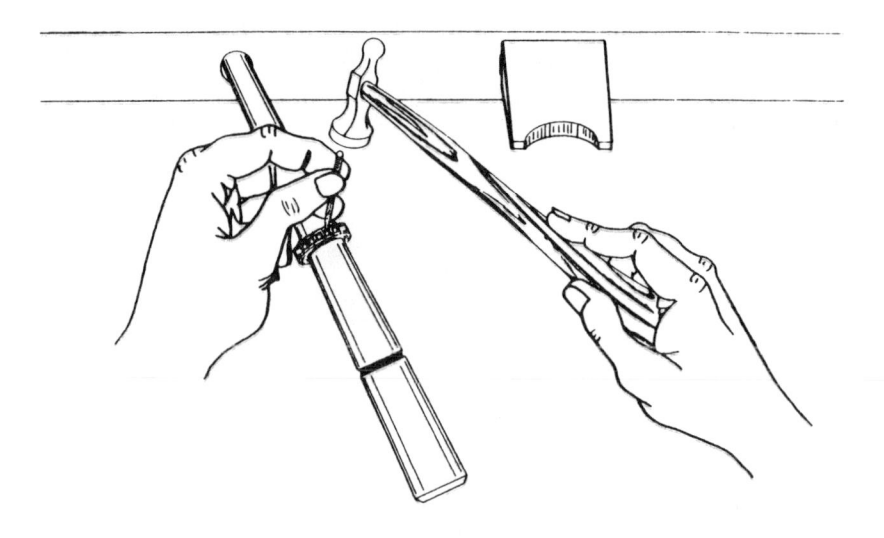

Fig. 1.33 Shows the recommended position to hold a chasing hammer and tapping tool.

Fixtures For Hammering/Tapping

The mounting being secured by a hammering technique has to be held in a fixture that will allow it to withstand vibration without collapsing or shifting. A number of fixtures are available including a mandrel, Bench-Mate™, padded vice, and engraving block (See Fig. 1.34). If the jewelry piece is a strongly constructed ring, either fixture is suitable provided the culets of the diamonds do not extend into the finger area. In that case the use of a mandrel might be eliminated (the diamonds will chip). If the diamonds do protrude too far then a grooved mandrel may be considered if the groove will contain all of the diamonds. A diamond being hammer set should never extend to any fixture whether it is the diamond being secured at the time or not. The force developed by hammering is projected to all parts of the mounting. Fragile rings and other jewelry in the form of earrings, pendants, etc., require special attention. They have to be packed with diamond setters' cement, usually on a cement stick, then mounted into one of the clamping fixtures.

SECURE THE DIAMONDS 43

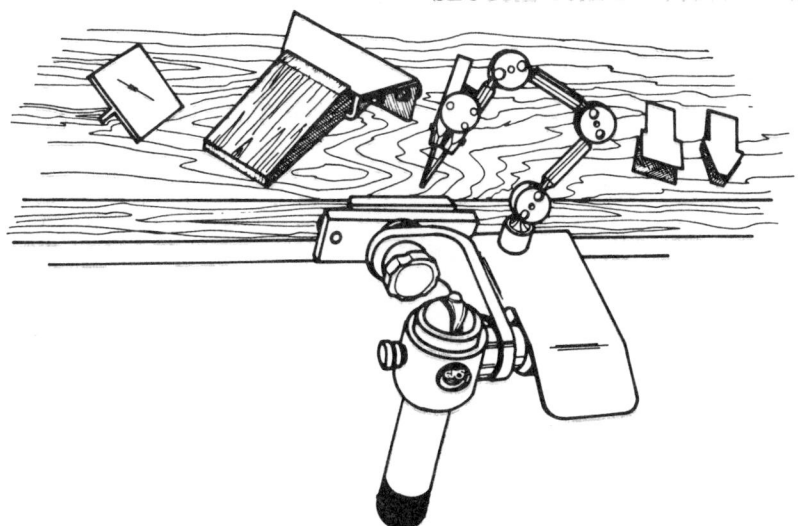

Fig. 1.34 BenchMate™ by GRS Engraving Products. A sturdy fixture that holds jewelry at multiple angles.

TESTING A DIAMOND FOR SECURITY

To determine if a diamond is tight, a few methods are suggested. One is to lightly grasp the girdle with small tweezers and attempt to turn the diamond. The lightest effort should be applied or else the diamond will become loose or chipped. Another method is to use a probing tool such as a graver or scriber (See Fig. 1.35). To check a diamond this way, caution must be exercised to avoid chipping it. Slide the tool down the crown of the diamond without pressure to the girdle, then up from the pavilion facets. If the diamond is loose, it will push down unnoticed but be seen moving when the tool raises up from the pavilion facet. One other method is safer but sometimes messier. It is done by simply pressing bees wax to the table facet of the diamond and trying to move it.

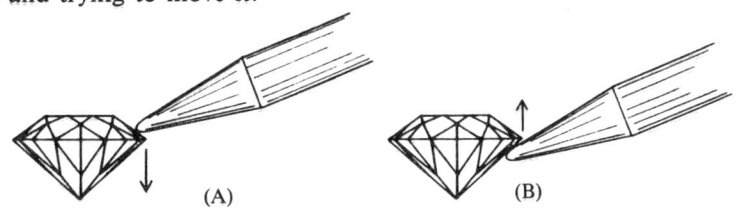

(A)   (B)

Fig. 1.35 Using a probing tool to test a diamond for security.
(A) Shows the tool sliding (without pressure) down the crown facets of a diamond.
(B) Shows the tool rising up (without pressure) from the pavilion facets of a diamond.
If the diamond moves it is loose.

44 SECURE THE DIAMONDS

The importance of having tight bearings is fully realized when diamonds are hammer set. Undercutting a channel is not mandatory, but it is helpful to keep the diamonds from bouncing out when the metal is hammered. Diamonds seated into a channel that has thin walls can be secured by the use of pliers as discussed earlier. When a channel is not undercut, the top of one side can first be hammered slightly over to provide a ledge. This is done with the diamonds removed from the bearings. Then the diamonds are re-seated and only the metal on the opposite side of the channel has to be hammered to tighten the diamonds. In other cases the diamonds might have to be secured one at a time by carefully alternating the hammering from opposite sides of the channel. Except in extreme instances, all the diamonds should be pre-tightened and assured of being favorably positioned before permanently securing them.

6

Finishing

Finishing is the concluding phase of channel setting. It is a sculpturing process to restore the mounting to an abrasion free design. A certain amount of metal will have to be removed from the mounting depending upon the irregularity incurred during the setting procedure. The tools used for finishing vary according to the shape of the metal and the amount of metal that needs to be removed in order to reveal the intended design. It is favorable to have a lot of metal to work with, but compensation techniques are available if necessary. After the complete form of the design is disclosed, the metal is trimmed to show detail. Then it is made smooth to prepare it for polishing. At the completion of the finishing phase, the jewelry should resemble what the diamond setter had envisioned since the layout phase.

REMOVE INDENTATIONS

The first objective toward finishing a channel set mounting is to remove indentations from the metal. Normally this can be done by filing or, less frequently, by burnishing. Filing is the easiest technique, partially because there is a vast selection of file shapes and sizes available that can be used for channel settings. Some of these include a variety of needle files with shapes for practically every conceivable contour, and flat hand files for long spans of metal. Burnishing, on the other hand, is a more vigorous finishing technique. It is an option that is taken when removing metal is not desirable. Neither filing nor burnishing can be singled out as the best all round technique to remove indentations. The use of each depends upon preference and the occurrence of particular conditions.

Filing

Filing to remove indentations in a mounting is a gradual process. Only a little metal is removed at a time to avoid removing too much. The objective is to reveal a uniform shape that is concealed within the metal. Performing the task is similar to the work of a sculpturer. Only the metal that does not pertain to the design is removed. First the tops of the channel are filed simultaneously with a flat hand file, or barrette needle file, to ensure a parallel surface (See Fig. 1.36 Line A). Be careful not to make contact with the diamonds. If contact cannot be avoided, then the top of each channel wall will have to be filed separately. Next, the sides of the channel are filed. A general consideration when filing these areas is that metal between the bases and top edges should eventually return to the original design (See Fig. 1.36 Line B). If the upper portion of one side is filed to remove dents, then for consistency purposes, the lower portion should also be filed.

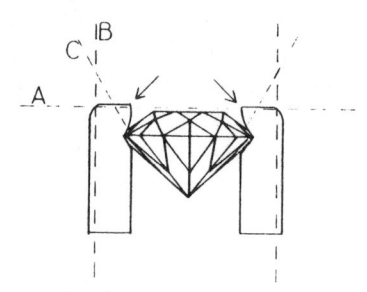

Fig. 1.36 Illustrates trimming requirements for a channel set diamond.
(A) Shows the top plane.
(B) Shows filing the side planes.
(C) Shows bevels from the crown facets of a diamond to the top of the channel walls.

Burnishing

Nearly any minor indentation in gold can be filled by burnishing. The technique is to rub the metal repeatedly in one direction with a narrow rounded blade. A round graver or a dull knife graver that will not cut into the metal can be used as well as a jewelers burnisher. Since gold is a malleable metal, it can be distributed from high to low spots without actually removing it. The process takes a considerable amount of time and effort; therefore its use is usually limited to smoothing metal that should not be thinned any further.

Some applications of burnishing include a situation where for one reason or another the security of the diamonds would be hampered if more metal were to be removed. Another reason for burnishing is when excessive filing would otherwise be necessary to remove a distortion in the metal. In that case the design could be affected. A final reason worthy of mention at this time, to burnish, is in the case when a diamond must be reset into a channel setting. After replacing the diamond, the metal is likely to be depressed because of the securing techniques. By burnishing, the metal from other areas can be moved to fill in that space.

TRIM THE DESIGN

Trimming is done to highlight the edges and borders of the design. Contours and special features should become distinct (See Fig. 1.37). Also, the metal overlapping the diamonds from the inner edges of the channel walls should be evenly distributed and equally extended over the diamonds on each side (See Fig. 1.36 Line C). Most of the metal that is not in contact with the diamonds can be trimmed uniformly by a suitably shaped needle file. The file need only brush the metal at a tangent angle just enough to remove sharp and ragged edges. Straight edges of metal along rows of diamonds can be beveled from the crown facets of the diamonds to the inside edge of the channel wall by a three corner needle file. When this is done, some metal might become flattened and stretch onto the diamonds. Those flakes of metal can be removed with a flat graver. A flat graver is also used to bevel securing metal that borders the diamonds in a circular channel. Trimming is a delicate process that should be done carefully, giving full attention to detail and removing as little metal as necessary.

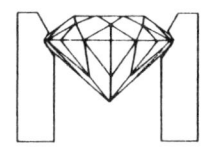

Fig. 1.37 Illustrates a channel set diamond trimmed symmetrically on both channel walls.

SMOOTH THE METAL

Smoothing metal is the final segment of the finishing phase. After finishing processes involving filing, burnishing, and engraving have been completed, the metal will be rough. It should then be made smooth in order to inspect the work for detail and to minimize polishing. This can be done with emery paper, polishing paper, and various shapes and sizes of rubber wheels. The selection of each depends upon the contour of the metal. Finishing materials such as these can also become abrasives if not used carefully. A touch and go technique to check the effects of each action is a must. There will be a lot of fine debris extruded from the materials combined with gold dust that will obstruct a clear view of the mounting. These should be brushed away continually during the smoothing process to inspect the metal. Lastly, minor imperfections in the design discovered at this time can usually be corrected by expanding on the same smoothing techniques.

SECTION II

Illustrated Channel Setting Procedures

    1 Basic Closed Channel
       Supplement for Fancy Cut Diamonds
    2 Basic Open Channel
    3 Curved Channels
    4 Tapered Channels
    5 Angular Channels
    6 Inlaid Channels
       (Round Diamonds)
    7 Inlaid Channels
       (Square Cut Diamonds)

Introduction

The objective of this section is to discuss and illustrate a variety of realistic channel setting procedures. The format is step by step as each phase is further reduced into fundamental activities. In actual practice a diamond setter will encounter straight, curvature, tapered, and angular channels. These designs, and different types such as open channels, closed channels, and inlaid channels are also presented. Although each design and type is unique to others, they are all elaborations of a basic channel setting procedure.

A learning program to channel set diamonds should include how to cut a channel. Many diamond setters seldom, if ever, are obligated to make a channel setting. This is not unusual, especially in larger jewelry production establishments where the task is given to the casting department or jewelry mechanic. Still, the diamond setter is required to have the knowledge and skills to perform the task. Every channel setting procedure includes phases to inspect, prepare, and frequently re-cut a channel. These techniques can be performed more effectively with the knowledge and skills of how a channel is made. For that reason the first procedure of this section emphasizes the techniques to make a channel setting from a solid band.

Continual changes is fashionable jewelry designs necessitate setting diamonds into various shapes and sizes of channels. Diamond setters are responsible for adapting skills and techniques to alternative procedures. This section, being attentive to those demands, increasingly introduces more complexity. A series of applications beginning with a basic channel setting gradually present topics with varying degrees of geometrics. The course concludes with higher echelons of channel setting. Illustrations show how to set diamonds into inlaid channels and channel setting fancy cut diamonds.

The selected channel setting procedures to follow are presented in a sequence from basic to more complex. Advanced techniques are increasingly

CHANNEL SETTING PROCEDURES

introduced. Some identical steps are repetitively mentioned among the topics. This is necessary in order to concentrate the discussions and illustrations of the entire channel setting procedure applicable to each topic. The previous section is intended to be used as an occasional reference source when particular problems arise. To continually divert from the written text to other sections would be distractive. In addition, the techniques and procedures described to channel set diamonds into each contour can be universally applied to a multitude of similar designs.

By the end of this section a prominent diamond setter should have obtained a thorough knowledge of channel setting procedures. When the techniques are actually applied to the workplace, the importance of each phase will be understood. Like all diamond setting, the success of each phase is dependent upon its subsequent phase. The possible channel configurations are unlimited; however, once the fundamentals are instilled, along with the optional techniques to deal with complex designs, there should be no drawback to any channel setting procedure. In order to understand how the steps of the procedure are interrelated, it is strongly recommended that this entire section be reviewed before attempting any channel setting task.

1

Basic Closed Channel

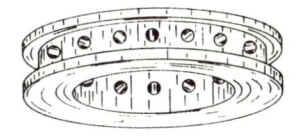

Channel setting diamonds normally begins with a mounting that has a pre-cut channel. The channel might or might not require some alteration before setting diamonds into it. Sometimes there is no channel at all. It is not unusual that the mounting is solid and the diamond setter, or jewelry mechanic, has to cut the channel. Even if the diamond setter is never required to cut a channel, the technique is important to learn. The most basic channel setting procedures are adaptable for various sizes of diamonds. Within limits, the diamond setter must be able to proficiently make minor adjustments. The prerequisite is that the diamond setter knows how and has the skills to cut a channel from beginning to end.

This procedure emphasizes the skills necessary to cut a channel. Illustrations include showing a channel cut into a solid band and the diamond secured into an undercut bearing. It requires a layout, drilling, taper boring, reaming, and other channel setting techniques that involve the use of gravers. Any number of diamonds can be channel set into this type of mounting up to a complete eternity ring. For instruction purposes the discussion focuses on cutting a channel for five diamonds. If more diamonds are to actually be set, such as for an eternity ring, then the same procedure is merely extended.

STEP 1. Inspect the mounting. The illustrated mounting is a solid band (See Fig. 2.2). It is adaptable to a channel setting and a number of other diamond setting procedures. Examine the mounting for defects and other prior work done to it that might affect the quality and strength. Become familiar with all the characteristics that will, in part, determine what tools and techniques are most applicable to channel set diamonds into it.

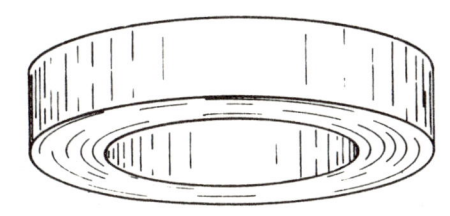

Fig. 2.2 Shows a solid band adaptable for channel setting.

54 BASIC CLOSED CHANNEL

STEP 2. Inspect the diamonds. Use a 7X-10X eye loupe to search for flaws, chips, and other inperfections. Report defects to the appropriate authority whether that person is an immediate supervisor or customer. Studying the characteristics of the diamonds is also important in order to discover defects that might require special attention later in the procedure.

STEP 3. Check to see if the diamonds can be channel set into the mounting. This need only be a brief test to compare the width and depth of the diamonds to the mounting. Only one diamond needs to be tested unless there is a noticeable difference in size. If the diamonds differ in size, then others will have to be tested as well.

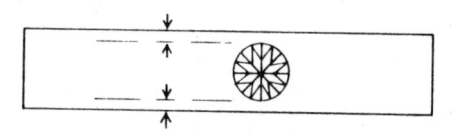

Fig. 2.3 Shows a diamond positioned table facet down on a solid band during the inspection phase to see if there will be enough metal at each side to secure the diamonds.

Compare the width of the mounting to the diamonds by placing one diamond table facet down and centered on top of the metal (See Fig. 2.3). Diamonds in the vicinity of .03ct.-.10ct. laid out on a solid plate should have at least about one-half millimeter of metal remaining on each side. That metal is used to secure the diamonds. More will be needed to cut the bearings. The requirement for smaller and larger diamonds will vary slightly.

To test the depth, hold one diamond via bees wax to the side of the mounting at an approximate level where it will eventually be seated. The seating level should be about one and one-half times the distance from the girdle of the diamond to the height of its table facet (See Fig. 2.4). At that level the culet should not extend below the bottom of the mounting.

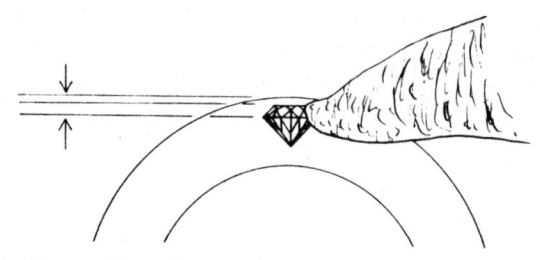

Fig. 2.4 Shows a diamond held by bees wax to the side of a solid band to check if the diamonds can be set below the surface. The culets should not protrude through the underside.

STEP 4. Prepare the mounting for the layout. Look at the top surface of the mounting from both an end and a side view. It should be smooth and planed according to the design. Often a bar of metal such as this will be

BASIC CLOSED CHANNEL 55

slanted or wavy. A fine casting will probably not require more than a light sanding with emery paper. In other cases file the top with long, arching strokes that conform to the design. Use a fine cut-flat hand file until file marks cover the entire surface. Depressions in the metal will be noticed immediately by where the file does not cut.

STEP 5. Emery the file marks. Use NO. 2 emery paper wrapped on a flat emery stick. This has to be done so that layout marks to be engraved later will be distinguishable.

STEP 6. Arrange the diamonds in order of size on a diamond tray. Use bees wax or tweezers to handle them. By having the diamond tray on the bench pin, and the diamonds resting on pavilion facets in the tray, the diameters of the diamonds can be compared. Place the diamonds in line with the tops facing in view. Shift the largest diamonds to the center with others tapered to both ends of the line to the smallest diamonds. There might be very little variation in size, but the detection at this stage will make a significant difference during later phases. Maintain that order throughout the procedure.

STEP 7. Rub a film of bees wax on top of the mounting. Apply only enough to cause the table facets of the diamonds to adhere to it. This will keep the diamonds stabilized while they are being laid out.

STEP 8. Place the diamonds on the mounting table facets down. Transfer one diamond at a time to its respective location on the mounting from the order that is in the diamond tray. Use bees wax to pick up the diamonds by touching it to the culets.

STEP 9. Adjust the spacing among diamonds and between the edges of the metal. A flat graver can be used to do this. As each diamond is arranged in position, press the bottom of the graver gently on the culet. The pressure will be projected to the table facet causing it to adhere to the wax and temporarily stabilize the diamond in that position. A good view to accurately space the diamonds is looking straight down to them and the top of the mounting.

Since the surface is an arch, there has to be a small space between the diamonds on the layout because they will tend to join closer when seated to a lower depth. Diamonds being channel set into a level bar of metal may be laid out girdle to girdle if it is feasible.

STEP 10. Use a scriber or pointed graver to mark the metal at the girdles of the diamonds. It is important to keep in mind that these first markings are made only to find the center drilling locations. The channel should not be cut to those lines. Actual channel cutting borders will be engraved later. Be as specific as possible giving very little tolerance. A direct top view is necessary to accurately mark between the diamonds and along the girdles

56 BASIC CLOSED CHANNEL

near the edges of the metal (See Fig. 2.5). If there is a lot of space between diamonds, there may be continuous lines across the plate. Otherwise, make a tick mark from the edges of the metal to the point where the diamonds join.

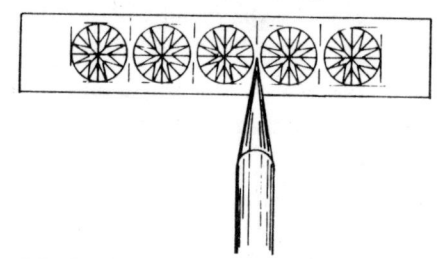

Fig. 2.5 Shows a scriber marking the positions of the diamonds during the layout.

STEP 11. Remove the diamonds one at a time from the mounting. As each diamond is removed place it back into the diamond tray in the same order as before.

STEP 12. Remove the bees wax from the mounting and diamonds. The wax can be wiped off of the mounting with a cloth. Removing it from the diamonds is more tedious. One method is to rub each diamond between the thumb and forefinger. Another way is to stretch a cloth over a flat surface such as the bench pin. Then tumble each diamond back and forth over it by pressing on the diamond with a finger tip.

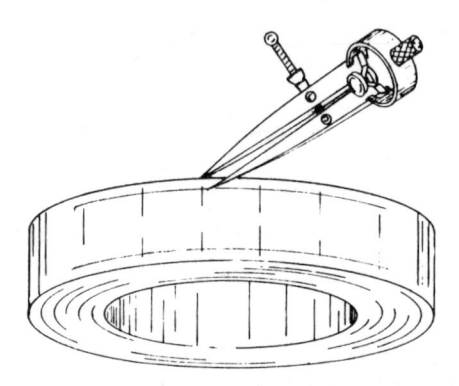

Fig. 2.6 Shows dividers used to extend layout markings.

STEP 13. With the diamonds removed, extend the marking to clarify them. One important aspect is to continue the edge lines. This can be done uniformly with dividers (See Fig. 2.6). Other engravings require freehand skills. Extend all the lines to make the layout as clear as possible.

BASIC CLOSED CHANNEL 57

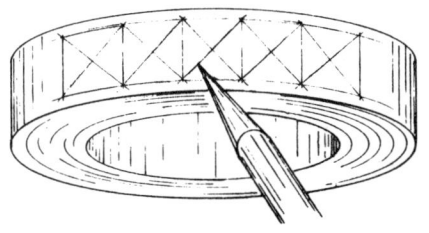

Fig. 2.7 Using a scriber to engrave diagonal lines to find centers for drilling.

STEP 14. Engrave diagonal lines between the corners of the markings to find center points for drilling (See Fig. 2.7). To ensure that the center points are in a straight row, engrave a center line. To do this, adjust dividers by trial and error at any point that is equal distance between the edges of the metal. When the center is found, use that divider adjustment to engrave a center line on which all the holes will be drilled. (See Fig. 2.8). This is done by bracing one point of the dividers against either edge of the metal while drawing the other point on the top surface.

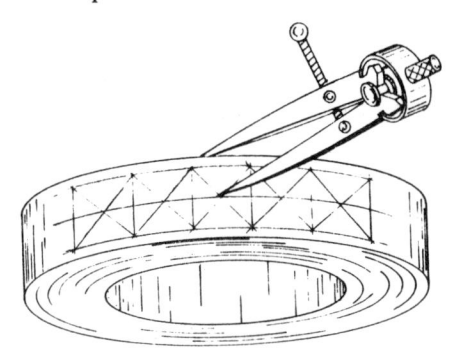

Fig. 2.8 Shows dividers used to engrave a center line for drilling holes.

STEP 15. Indent starter holes for drilling at each center marking. A center punch or a round graver can be used to do this. If a round graver is used, pick a tiny bit of metal from opposite directions at each center point.

STEP 16. Drill the holes. Use an approximate NO. 60-65 size twist drill. It is important to keep the holes centered until they break through the underside of the metal. For this to happen the drilling must be done perpendicular to the mounting at each center point (See Fig. 2.9). During the first couple millimeters that the drill is cutting, continually check the drill shaft from the end and side view of the mounting. The plate metal for channel setting in this case will be thick, so occasionally remove the drill to submerge the tip into cooling oil.

58 BASIC CLOSED CHANNEL

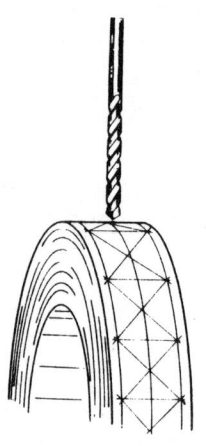

Fig. 2.9 Shows a twist drill positioned perpendicular to the contour of the mounting.

STEP 17. Taper bore one hole. This will be a reference from which others will copy later. Taper boring is done to excavate metal uniformly and centered at each of the diamonds' locations. Use a bud bur, or similar type of bur that is about two-thirds the diameter of the diamond. The bud bur size is deceiving to look at, so measure it with a millimeter degree gauge to be sure.

Taper bore the one hole centered between the two edge lines. The bur, being two-thirds the diameter of the diamond, should not be large enough to cut to the lines. Use an eye judgment to center the bore. The extremity of depth is not important as long as the bur does not project through the underside of the plate. That will distort the metal there and restrict adjustments later. However, it is favorable that the widest part of the bur extend at least to a depth that is twice the distance between the girdle of the diamond to the height of its table facet (See Fig. 2.10).

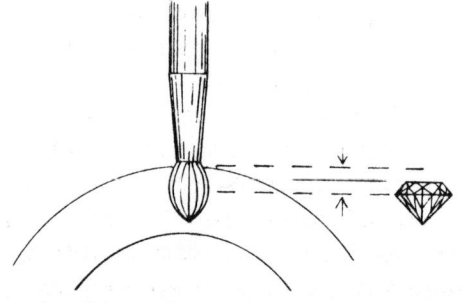

Fig. 2.10 Shows the minimum depth to taper bore a hole. The widest part of the bur approaches a depth that is twice the distance from the girdle of the diamond to the height of its table facet.

BASIC CLOSED CHANNEL 59

Remember, the first taper bore is a test and sample from which others will follow. While boring, occasionally remove the bur to compare it to the diamond to see that the bore is not being cut too large and that it is centered within the two edge lines. Again, the taper bore should not extend to those lines.

STEP 18. When one taper bore is satisfactory in depth and centered, use dividers to engrave cutting borders for the remaining taper bores. This is done by adjusting the dividers from the edge of the plate to the rim of the bore. Then engrave the borders along the plate from both edges using that divider adjustment (See Fig. 2.11).

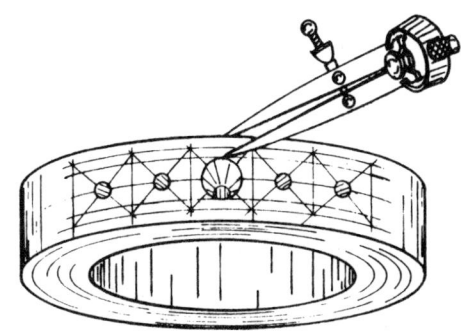

Fig. 2.11   After one taper bore is cut, dividers are used to engrave lines from those dimensions to guide other taper bores.

STEP 19. Taper bore the remaining holes to the same depth, and use the new border markings to keep the bores centered and in line. It will help to bore each hole a little at a time from one to another to keep them equally spaced. If necessary the holes can be pulled to any direction by tilting the bud bur.

STEP 20. Ream the holes. Reaming provides some relief and dimension to cutting the channel. Use a H.S. setting bur because it leaves a straight bore and a vertex in the metal. Straight bores serve as boundaries to cutting the width of the channel, and the distinctive vertexes show the depth to cut the basin. The tapered section of the H.S. setting bur that cuts into the basin conforms to the pavilions of the diamonds ensuring that they will not be blocked.

Since this particular channel will be undercut, the distance between the walls must be narrower than the diamonds. The recommended channel width in this case is three-fourths the diameter of the diamonds being set. Use a H.S. setting bur that size. It should be just a little larger than the taper bored holes. Later the channel will be cut to the rims of the reamed holes leaving just enough metal to cut a bearing into each channel wall. To avoid staggering the reams, engrave two parallel lines on the plate with dividers to mark

60 BASIC CLOSED CHANNEL

off their diameter just as was done for the taper bores. That will help to keep the reams in line and consequently the channel.

In order to obtain an ideal channel effect, the basin should be lower than the girdles of the diamonds after they are set. The diamonds will be seated to a level where the table facets are below the surface of the metal. That depth is about one and one-half times the height that the table facets are from the girdle facets; therefore, the basin level as shown by the vertexes cut by the setting bur should be a minimum of twice the distance between the girdles to the height of the table facets (See Fig. 2.12).

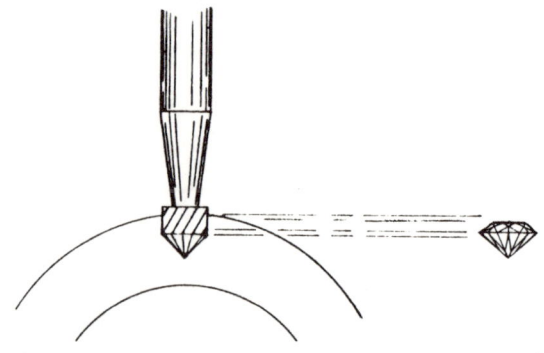

Fig. 2.12 Holes are reamed by a H.S. setting bur to a depth that is twice the distance from the girdles of the diamonds to the height of their table facets.

STEP 21. Begin rough cutting the channel with a piercing saw or knife graver straight along the edges of the reamed holes. Do not cut beyond the diameter of the reams nor deeper than their vertexes (See Fig. 2.13). It is better to leave a visible trace of the reams on each wall to ensure that the width of the channel will not be cut too wide. Later more metal will be removed when the channel is trimmed to the appropriate width.

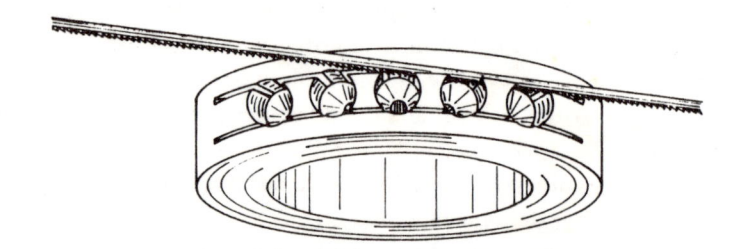

Fig. 2.13 Shows a piercing saw cutting the metal just within the edges of the reamed holes, and to the basin level, to begin rough cutting the channel.

STEP 22. Remove the metal between the side cuts to the basin. This can be done by a number of means including a flat graver, square needle file,

BASIC CLOSED CHANNEL   61

and wheel bur (See Fig. 2.14). Another handy tool that could be used to cut the channel can be made from a large setting bur by grinding off its lower portion. Remember to leave a visible trace of the reams on the walls when doing this to avoid cutting the channel too wide.

Fig. 2.14   Using a wheel bur to remove metal between the saw cuts to the channel basin.

The ring in the illustrations is shown having five diamonds set into it. In such a case the metal at the ends of the channel could be tapered or squared from the basin to the surface of the plate. If an eternity channel were being set, then the basin would be continuous. Do not cut through the edges of the plate because at some future time a customer might want to add diamonds to the channel.

STEP 23. Plane the basin and inner walls of the channel. Now the traces of the reams may be removed. A medium cut-square needle file can be used to remove rough cuts on the basin if it will fit into the channel. Bur cuts and other abrasions are usually filed from the inside walls in this type of channel with a barrette needle file. The channel walls should become straight and equal in thickness on both sides.

STEP 24. Inspect the channel for appropriate dimensions. First place one diamond on top of the channel and centered between the walls. Some experience is necessary to visualize if the extension of the diamond over the channel walls is sufficient. Generally, for a round diamond, if the channel width is cut to three-fourths the diameter of the diamonds, then each wall should contain one-eighth the diameter of the diamond. Next, tilt the diamond into one side of the channel to a point where the girdle is at the proposed bearing level. The reamed holes below the basin should be large enough that the culet will not be blocked by the basin. Also, the opening of the tapered cuts in the basin that were made by the setting bur should extend to the side walls; otherwise, the diamonds might not set low enough in the channel, regardless of the bearing depth. It is usually necessary to recut the holes in the basin with the setting bur after trimming the channel. Finally, make sure that the entire length of the basin where the diamonds will set is at a uniform depth and the inside walls are perpendicular to the basin.

STEP 25. Smooth the channel. Unsightly areas might be permanent after the diamonds are secured. Use a large flat rubber wheel to remove file marks, etc., from the basin and a knife edge pumice wheel to smooth the inner walls. Pre-polish the channel if it is feasible.

STEP 26. Mark the top on one side of the channel at several locations. These marks will be a constant reminder that it is the side to be undercut. During the process of cutting bearings and checking the work, it is easy to become disoriented as to what side of the channel is being undercut. Marking the metal is important because securing the diamonds into an undercut channel requires a different treatment to each side of the channel.

STEP 27. Select a hart bur to cut the bearings. At first try a hart bur that is slightly smaller in diameter than the diamond being set there. Later the exact size can be used if necessary. A bur often cuts a larger bearing than its size. It is extremely important that the bearing is not cut too large. If there is any doubt, use a millimeter degree gauge to compare the measurements of the diamond and the bur selected.

STEP 28. Cut the bearings. Begin each bearing by placing the hart bur into position without applying power. First tilt the bur into the channel centered between border markings at the side to be undercut. Place the cutting edge of the bur at the proposed bearing level. This is about one and one-half times the distance from the girdle of the diamond to the height of its table facet. The placement can be checked by holding the bur steady while looking at the position of the cutting edge from an end view of the channel. Although the bur is tilted into one side, another view of the bur is also necessary to ensure that the bur is not slanted towards either end of the channel.

Apply power to the bur slowly until it begins to cut into the metal. This often takes a number of trials to re-check the position of the bur and the cut. The cut should be level, to the right depth, and centered between border markings. When the bur begins to cut into the metal and can be held steady in position, push it directly into the wall. Cut to a distance that is equal to the distance that the bur will cut into the opposite channel wall. While the hart bur is undercutting one wall, pivot it at the same time to make a vertical cut down the opposite side of the channel (See Fig. 2.15). Gradually increase the power as necessary to cut smoothly. Stop when the bur shaft is nearly

BASIC CLOSED CHANNEL 63

perpendicular to the channel. Later if the diamond will not set level because of a high vertical cut bearing, the bur can be brought to a more upright position.

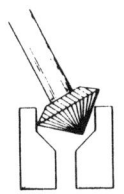

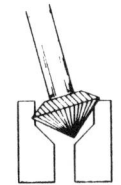

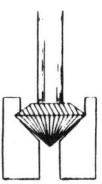

Fig. 2.15 Using a hart bur to undercut one wall of the channel while vertically cutting the opposite wall.

STEP 29. Inspect the bearing by attempting to seat the diamond into it. The diamond should set level with its table facet below the top of the channel. Check this from an end and side view. If the diamond will not fit into the bearing then either use a larger hart bur or enlarge the bearing by pushing the same bur a little farther into the undercut. If the diamond will not set low enough, the basin might have to be cut lower.

STEP 30. When the precise method to cut the bearings into this particular channel is established, cut the remaining bearings. Remove the seated diamond first to avoid chipping it or dulling the bur. Keep in mind that the size of the diamonds will vary. Each diamond might require a slightly larger or smaller bearing.

STEP 31. Seat the diamonds. As the bearing for each diamond is cut, that diamond should be trial seated then removed and placed back in order on the diamond tray. When all the bearings are satisfactory, clean the diamonds and brush debris from the mounting. Then seat the diamonds permanently.

STEP 32. Check the overall seating arrangement. The diamonds should be seated to a uniform depth with the table facets on a consistent plane. Also, the spacing between each diamond should be equal.

STEP 33. Secure the diamonds. The technique described here to secure the diamonds at first requires slimline-chain nose pliers. The innerface of the jaws are flat, thereby minimizing distortion to the sides of the mounting.

Place one jaw of the pliers upright and flat against the outside of the channel wall that is undercut. Position the other jaw outside the upper edge of the opposite channel wall (See Fig. 2.16). When pressure is applied, the metal that extends above the diamonds on the channel that is not undercut should bend to secure the diamonds. To do this squeeze the pliers a little at each diamond. Then go back and squeeze the metal between the diamonds. Work the metal gradually while moving the pliers along the channel. Watch the metal as it bends, being careful not to apply excessive pressure. The metal

64 BASIC CLOSED CHANNEL

does not have to bend onto the crown facets of the diamond to secure them. The metal tightening against the girdle facets should be sufficient.

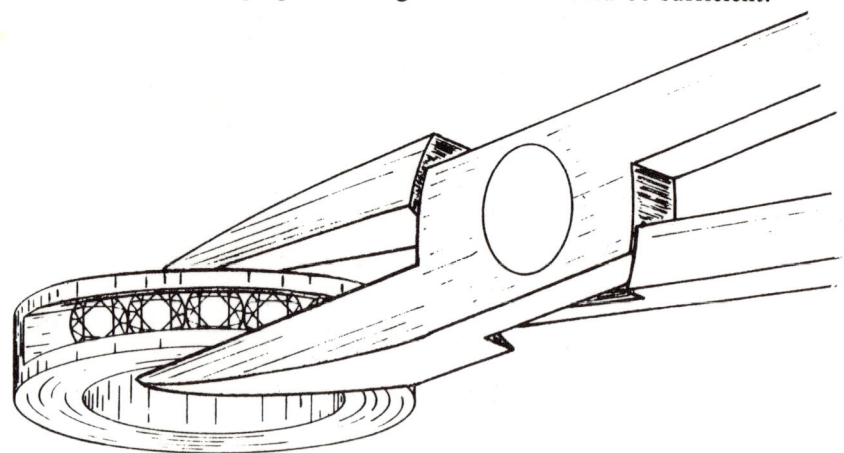

Fig. 2.16 Shows chain nose pliers used to secure the diamonds. One jaw is used to brace the undercut side while metal from the non-undercut wall is bent to secure the diamonds.

STEP 34. Bend the metal onto the diamonds from the undercut channel wall. This might seem unnecessary because of the undercut, but it is a part of the procedure to ensure that the metal is against the diamonds. It is merely a re-enactment that was done with pliers to the opposite side of the channel. Be very careful not to apply too much pressure because, unless the diamonds are loose, it is not likely that the metal can be seen moving.

STEP 35. Check to see that the metal on both sides of the channel extends over the diamonds. It is not vital for security that the extension is far just so a portion of the girdle facets are not visible at each side from a direct top view.

STEP 36. Close the gaps between the crown facets of the diamonds and the metal that extends over them. This is a distractive area that is attended to primarily for cosmetic purposes. The diamonds are usually quite secure at the girdles in spite of the gaps, if they were seated snugly to begin with. The technique requires a tapping tool, chasing hammer, and fixture to hold the ring. The use of a mandrel is discussed, but a BenchMate™ padded vice, or engraving block could also be used. If the task is considered to be unnecessary, then either apply it in part or eliminate it and continue with the next step.

The side of the channel that is not undercut is tapped first. Assuming that the diamonds do not protrude to the finger area, place the ring on a mandrel with the undercut side of the channel nearer the wide end. From that position movement of the metal can be seen as it is tapped, and the

BASIC CLOSED CHANNEL 65

hammering is less likely to force the ring loose on the mandrel. If there is a lot of metal above the diamonds, it can be filed a little to provide a flat tapping surface. The flattening will help to keep the tapping tool from slipping. Also, the metal being thinned somewhat will be easier to tap down.

Since the channel metal has been bent over by the pliers, the tapping can begin with the tapping tool held in a nearly upright position. Hold the tapping tool with the tip flat and centered on the metal (See Fig. 2.17). The diameter of the tip should be about one millimeter to minimize indentations and allow an unobstructed view.

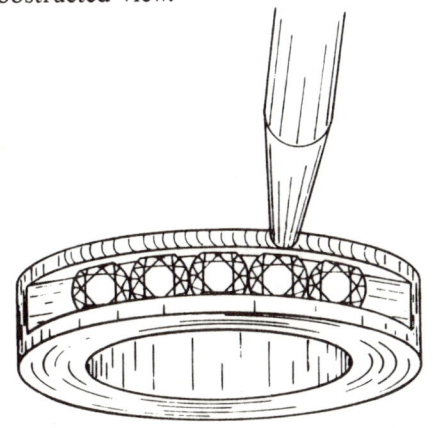

Fig. 2.17 Using a tapping tool to bend the metal farther to the diamonds.

Hit the end of the tapping tool squarely with the face of the chasing hammer. Use steady quick strokes rather than forceful percussions. Keep the tapping tool moving along the metal and occasionally turn the mandrel to position the ring. Do not tap the metal continuously in one area. This could cause a diamond to chip or severely indent the metal. Also, do not try to close all the metal completely to the diamonds. Much of the over-hanging metal will be removed later anyway when it is trimmed. Excessive hammering during this stage is very risky.

Reverse the ring on the mandrel to repeat the technique to the undercut side of the channel. Use even less force than what was applied to the side that was not undercut. The girdles of the diamonds are wedged in the undercut bearings and will chip easily. Undercut metal is lightly tapped to ensure that the diamonds are tightly secured. When tapping the undercut side of the channel, the metal might not be seen moving except in areas where there is a loose diamond.

STEP 37. Remove indentations. Use a fine to medium cut-flat hand file or a barrette needle file. First check to see if both sides of the channel can be filed together. To do this, place the file across the channel, and from an

66 BASIC CLOSED CHANNEL

end view of the mounting determine if the diamonds are well below the surface. The file could loosen or chip diamonds. Otherwise, file one side of the channel at a time. Do not try to remove all indentations if the metal is thin. More metal will be removed later by emery paper.

STEP 38. File the sides of the mounting from the finger area to the top edge of the channel. The purpose is to remove indentations caused by the pliers. If the metal is thin, it might have to be beveled slightly or emeried. This is undesirable because it will leave both sides of the mounting rounded, but sometimes must be done to ensure that the metal will maintain strength. Preferably the sides of the mounting are shaped to the original design.

STEP 39. Remove all file marks and remaining indentations in the mounting. Use NO. 2 emery paper wrapped on an emery stick. Do not depend upon polishing or another craftsman to do this work. The closer to perfection that the diamond setter can perform, the less the chances are for others tampering with one's craft.

STEP 40. Trim the channel. Use a NO. 6 three corner-needle file to trim the inner edges of the channel. This is the metal that extends over the crown facets of the diamonds. Do not remove a lot of metal, just enough to slightly bevel it from the diamonds and to straighten it (See Fig. 2.18.). Use long gentle strokes in one direction. If there is very little metal to trim, or a file cannot be used, use a flat graver with a polished tip. Afterwards smooth the bevel with a knife edge pumice wheel.

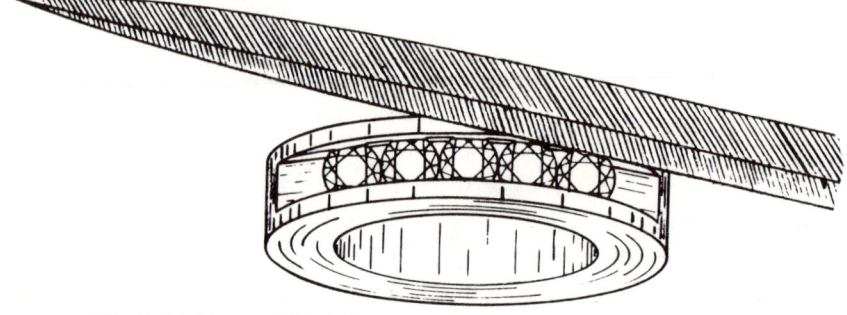

Fig. 2.18 Shows a NO. 6 three corner-needle file used to trim the metal that extends over the crown facets of the diamonds.

STEP 41. Remove sharp edges from the mounting. Use a NO. 6 barrette needle file lightly over areas such as the outer edges of the channel. If a bevel is necessary to straighten the edges, be sure that the width of the metal and design is equal on both sides of the channel.

STEP 42. Smooth the mounting. To smooth the top of the channel walls, use either NO. 4/0 polishing paper wrapped on an emery stick or a large rubber wheel flattened at the edge. (The edge of a rubber wheel can be flattened

BASIC CLOSED CHANNEL 67

or sharpened by rotating it against a coarse file). Apply long brushing strokes being careful not to damage the metal. Use NO. 4/0 polishing paper to smooth the sides of the mounting.

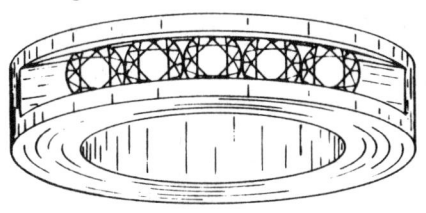

Fig. 2.19   Shows round diamonds set into a basic closed channel.

SUPPLEMENT

Auxillary Illustrations to Set Square Cut Diamonds into a Basic Closed Channel

A procedure to set square cut diamonds into a channel that has a basin can be similar in many respects to that of round diamonds. There are, of course, some differences but they pertain more to additional tasks rather than to deviations in those techniques. The mounting and diamonds are inspected and compared by the same methods and the principles of the layout are similar. Also securing the diamonds and finishing are technically interchangeable between channel setting round and fancy cut diamonds. Cutting the bearings into a channel for either round or square faceted diamonds can be done with gravers if preferred. Gravers are recommended to cut bearings for square faceted diamonds. When a basin is involved, further attention has to be given if it is to contain straight faceted pavilions. The following series of illustrations show the differences to channel setting square cut diamonds into the same mounting as previously discussed. Other than the basin is cut to contain the special features of a square cut diamond, the procedure is generally the same.

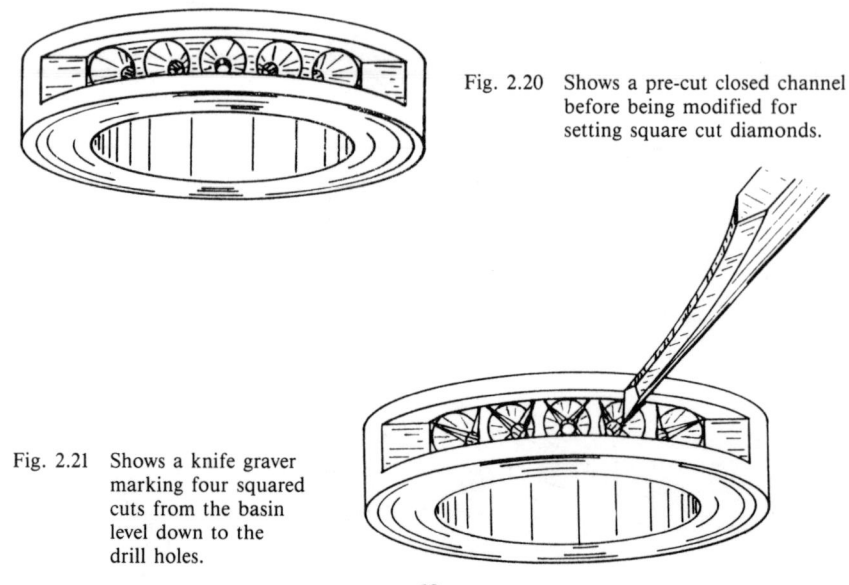

Fig. 2.20 Shows a pre-cut closed channel before being modified for setting square cut diamonds.

Fig. 2.21 Shows a knife graver marking four squared cuts from the basin level down to the drill holes.

SUPPLEMENT FOR FANCY CUT DIAMONDS

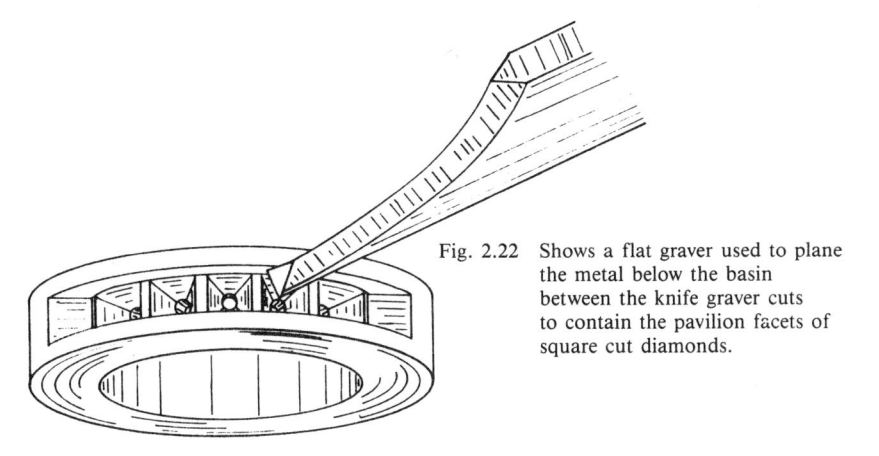

Fig. 2.22 Shows a flat graver used to plane the metal below the basin between the knife graver cuts to contain the pavilion facets of square cut diamonds.

Fig. 2.23 Shows a flat graver used to undercut one side of the channel wall.

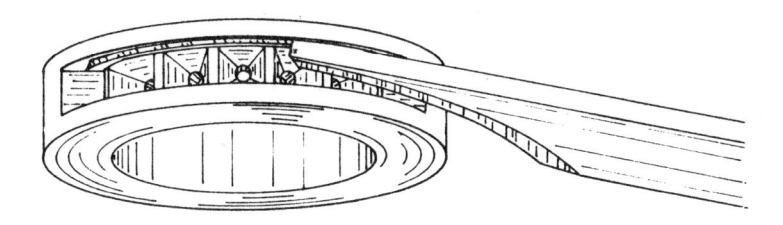

Fig. 2.24 Sectional view of undercut and vertical cut bearings for a square cut diamond. The top dotted line represents the basin.

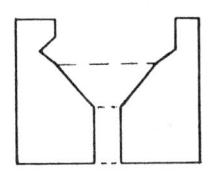

Fig. 2.25 Shows five square cut diamonds secured into a closed channel.

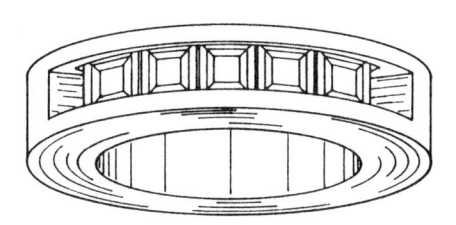

2

Basic Open Channel

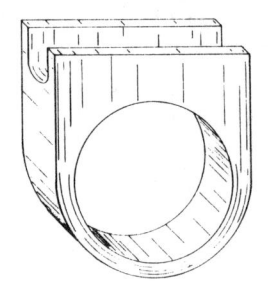

An open channel is a type that has the walls attached well below the diamonds or at the ends of the channel. This section describes and illustrates setting diamonds into a basic open channel. There is no basin to contend with, the top of the channel is straight and level, and the walls are narrow. The objective of the design is to set the diamonds with the table facets on a level plane. It is not difficult, but does involve tedious work with close tolerances. Many of the same techniques to set diamonds into a basic open channel are used in procedures of the most exquisite channel designs. Once these skills are developed, they can be adapted to other variations of channel setting.

STEP 1. Inspect the mounting. Be concerned about the quality and structure of the mounting. Severely pitted metal and other defects could affect the procedure. Knowing that these exist beforehand is helpful to avoid problems later. Awareness of the structure is important because the mounting will be subjected to some abuse during the procedure. Weak mountings might have to be supported with diamond setters cement when performing certain techniques, or special fixtures might be necessary. If no immediate action is warranted, then at least a mental note should be made of the faults and any others that are discovered.

STEP 2. Inspect the diamonds. The condition of the diamonds will have a direct effect on the manner that they are set. Imperfections should be noted at this time and reported if any are severe. Do not accept responsibility for the diamonds without first thoroughly inspecting them. All of the diamonds should be the same size for this mounting. Some corrective action can be taken later by trimming during the finishing phase. If any diamond is excessively larger or smaller, it will stand out in the finished product.

BASIC OPEN CHANNEL 71

STEP 3. Prepare the mounting for setting. Check to be sure that both channel walls are parallel and have no depressions. This can be done by filing the top of the channel walls evenly with a fine cut-flat hand file. Low areas will not be covered by file marks. Look at the channel from an end view to see if either wall is noticeably lower than the other. Also, look at the mounting from a side view to see if it is symmetric to the design (See Fig. 3.2).

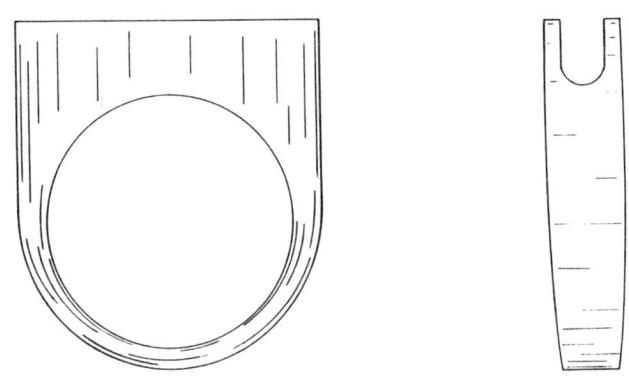

Fig. 3.2 Shows a side and end view of a basic open channel.

If the top of the channel walls are parallel, then only a light filing is necessary, otherwise more metal will have to be removed from the higher wall. Once the tops of the walls are both the same height, file them simultaneously until the file marks cover the surfaces with one pass. This will ensure that any depressions in the metal are eliminated. Then file 45°-90° to those file marks to make sure that the first filing was made level to the surface. Afterwards, emery the top of the channel to remove file marks.

STEP 4. Check the channel width. Space the diamonds evenly and centered on the channel walls with the table facets down. The width of the channel between the walls should be about three-fourths the diameter of the diamonds (See Fig. 3.3). If the diamonds extend over the edges of the channel, the walls can be spread within reason by flat nose pliers. Conversely, the walls can be closed if they are too wide. Later the bearings will be cut into each wall to a distance that is one-eighth the diameter of the diamonds.

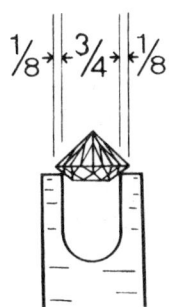

Fig. 3.3 Shows a round diamond positioned table facet down on an open channel during the inspecting phase. The channel should be about three-fourths the diameter of the diamond. Bearings are cut into each channel wall to a distance equal to about one-eighth the diameter of the diamond.

72 BASIC OPEN CHANNEL

STEP 5. Mark the locations of the diamonds. Look straight down to the channel and diamonds from a top view for better visibility and accuracy. Use a pointed graver, or a scriber, to scratch border lines between each diamond and at the ends of the channel (See Fig. 3.4). Then remove the diamonds to extend any marks that are not clear. The diamonds should be kept in order of size in a diamond tray. By this time it should be known exactly where each diamond will be set.

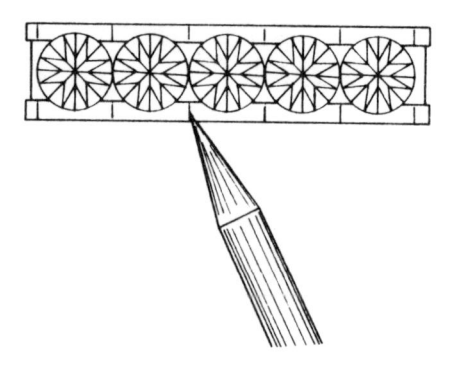

Fig. 3.4 Using a scriber to mark the layout locations of the diamonds.

STEP 6. Select a hart bur to cut the bearings. Since one side of the channel will be undercut, the hart bur is ideal. Its diameter should be just a little smaller than the diamonds. Sometimes, especially when undercutting, a hart bur will cut a bearing larger than the bur size. If the smaller bur turns out to be too small, then the exact size bur as the diamond can be used later. At least with pre-cut bearings the exact size bur will cut with less stress, thereby perform with increased accuracy.

STEP 7. Cut the first bearing by trial and error to serve as an example for the others. Tilt the bur into the side of the channel that is to be undercut. The bur should be centered between border markings with the cutting edge at the appropriate bearing level (See Fig. 3.5A). A good bearing depth for a channel set diamond is about one and one-half times the distance between the girdle to the height of its table facet. When the bur begins to rotate steadily between the borders, slowly increase the power while pushing it into the channel wall. At first concentrate on the side of the channel that is being undercut. After a small amount of metal is cut, remove the bur to check the cut. The beginning of the bearing should be straight along the proposed bearing line and at the correct depth. Make corrections as needed by re-positioning the bur.

BASIC OPEN CHANNEL 73

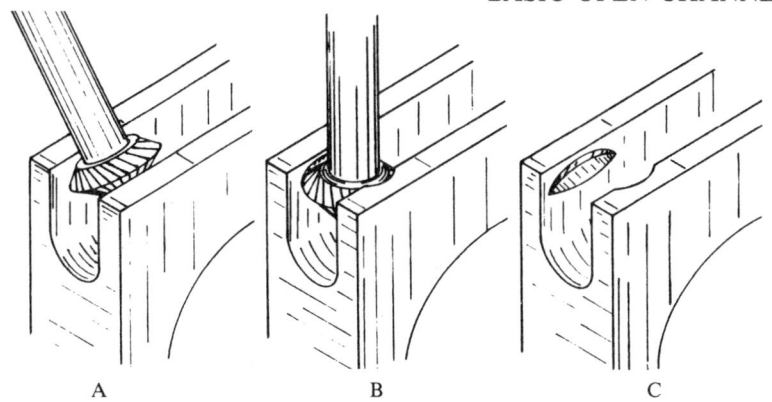

Fig. 3.5 Shows a method to undercut bearings into an open channel using a hart bur.

To complete the bearing, set the hart bur into the channel in the adjusted position. Gradually increase the power to medium speeds as needed to cut the metal. At the same time that one wall is being undercut, pivot the bur to cut vertically down the opposite wall (See Fig. 3.5B). When the shaft of the bur is brought close to an upright position, the bearings should be level. Eventually, when the diamond is seated, it should extend to the same distance into each wall although they are cut differently.

STEP 8. Inspect the sample bearing. Before continuing check to see how the diamond fits into the bearing (See Fig. 3.6). It should slip snugly into the channel, seated level, and be seated below the surface of the channel walls. Check for these features from both an end and side view. If the bearing is too small, re-cut it with a larger bur, or use the same bur to cut farther into the undercut wall. Once the technique to cutting bearings for this particular channel is assured, the remaining bearings can be cut with confidence.

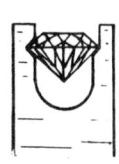

Fig. 3.6 Shows the end view of a properly seated diamond in an undercut-open channel.

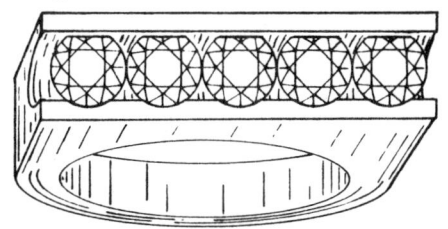

Fig. 3.7 Shows five equally spaced diamonds seated into an undercut-open channel.

STEP 9. Cut the remaining bearings. Do not leave any diamonds in the channel as subsequent bearings are being cut. They will only obstruct the view and possibly get chipped or dull the hart bur. Use the layout markings as a guide. Also, if the first bearing was cut with a smaller bur and enlarged by a larger bur, then the same technique should be done to cut the other bearings. Consistency is important in a straight channel with equal sized diamonds.

74 BASIC OPEN CHANNEL

Unless there is a problem with the first bearing, innovations should be reserved for more opportune times. There could be a slight size variation among the diamonds although they appear to be the same size. To avoid cutting any bearings too large, occasionally stop to inspect the fitting for the diamond that will be set into the bearing being cut.

STEP 10. Inspect the bearings. Brush the loose metal and other debris from the channel. Check the bearings for depth, uniform cuts, and levelness. One common problem is a double cut bearing that results from cutting a bearing too high then re-cutting it lower. This could cause a diamond to chip when it is secured. If a double cut bearing is inadvertent, then make a note of its location to give it extra care later when securing the diamond. An uneven cut and other bearing problems can usually be corrected by manipulating the hart bur and/or adjusting the channel with flat nose pliers.

STEP 11. Seat the diamonds. Place all of the diamonds into the channel by tilting them into the undercut wall and pushing them down on the opposite bearing. As each diamond is seated check it from the end and side views for level and depth. When corrections are necessary be sure to place the diamonds back into the respective bearings. The slightest variation in the size of diamonds will cause them to fit differently. When all of the diamonds are seated the table facets should all be on a level plane.

STEP 12. Check for equal spacing among the diamonds (See Fig. 3.7). At times a slightly larger diamond can be switched with a smaller one to open a space at one area and close a space at another area. If this is possible without sacrificing uneven or poorly seated diamonds, then it is better than recutting a bearing.

A bearing can be pulled toward or away from an adjacent bearing. This is done by placing the hart bur upright into the bearing and, while applying power, pushing it to the preferred direction. The result will be a diamond having a bearing that will allow it to slide in the channel. Special attention will have to be given when that diamond is secured. If pulling a bearing is done then the adjacent diamonds should be removed first, otherwise they will likely be hit by the bur.

STEP 13. Make final preparations to secure the diamonds. When all the diamonds are seated correctly, check to see that there is no debris on the diamonds or the metal. If the diamonds are seated snugly, the channel can be brushed lightly. Loosely seated diamonds can be stabilized for brushing by placing a thumb or forefinger on the diamonds at one side of the channel.

STEP 14. Secure the diamonds. Use slimline chain nose pliers. Brace one jaw of the pliers flatly against the undercut wall of the channel. Place the other jaw at the upper outer edge of the opposite channel wall (See Fig. 3.8).

BASIC OPEN CHANNEL 75

Hold the mounting and pliers in a position where the metal from the channel wall that is not undercut can be seen when it is bent onto the diamonds. Squeeze the pliers just enough at each diamond to see the metal move. Do this to the metal at each diamond, then check to see that the diamonds have remained level. If everything is satisfactory, then repeat the process. Eventually the entire upper channel wall, including the metal between the diamonds, should be bent slightly over the girdle facets of the diamonds.

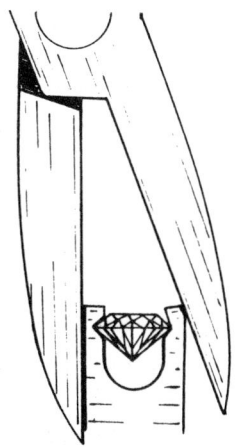

Fig. 3.8 Shows chain nose pliers used to secure a diamond into an undercut-open channel. One jaw braces the undercut wall flatly while the opposite wall is bent to secure the diamond.

Repeat the same technique to the undercut side of the channel. The metal might not be seen moving there, but for security assurance go through the technique in a similar manner. Undercut bearings are not always formed perfectly. Since the girdles of the diamonds are usually hidden, the simplest way to be sure the diamonds are secure from that side is to, as said, repeat the technique. A diamond can chip while doing this so be careful not to apply as much pressure than what was given to the opposite side of the channel.

STEP 15. Check the diamonds for security. First look at the mounting from a top view. Both channel walls should extend over the diamonds to a point where a portion of the girdles are not visible. If the metal does not cover adequately, it will have to be pulled farther by the pliers. Other tests can be done with tweezers or a probing tool. Be careful when using those methods because the diamonds could become loose or chipped. The safest test is done with bees wax by touching it to the diamonds to see if they are loose.

STEP 16. Tap the metal from both sides of the channel closer to the crown facets of the diamonds. Use a tapping tool and a lightweight chasing hammer. The tip of the tapping tool should taper to a flat circular surface with a diameter that is about one millimeter. A mandrel, whether grooved or ungrooved, can be used as a fixture to hold the mounting unless the diamonds extend under the channel to it. In that case an alternate clamping fixture should be used. Place the ring on the fixture to tap the side that is not undercut first. Tap the end of the tapping tool squarely with the chasing hammer. Keep the tip of the tool centered flat on the metal in an upright position and moving along the channel wall (See Fig. 3.9). Occasionally turn the ring to avoid tapping from an awkward position. Watch the metal as it moves closer to the diamonds and the effect that it has. Do not tap hard nor continuously in one area. Several light strikes offer a better chance to bend the metal evenly along the channel and avoid serious indentations or chipping the diamonds.

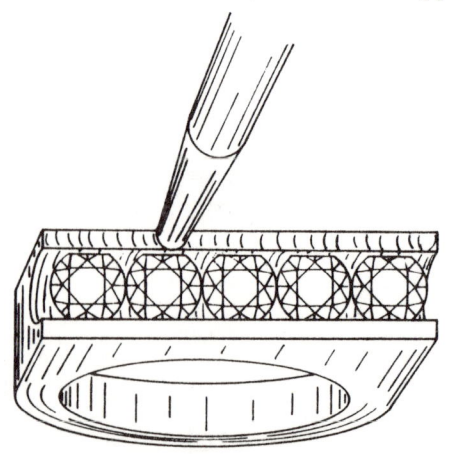

Fig. 3.9 Using a tapping tool to close the channel metal closer to the diamonds.

It is not necessary to close the metal completely to the diamonds because the edges will be trimmed back later during the finishing phase. If there is too much metal above the diamonds to bend easily, then file it down a little. The flattening will also help to control the movement of the tapping tool. After the non-undercut side of the channel is sufficiently bent to the diamonds, reverse the ring on the fixture to tap the undercut side likewise but with less force. The diamonds should be secure without doing any work to the undercut side; however, it is done for extra assurance and to create both sides of the channel symmetrically equal.

STEP 17. Remove indentations. First file the top of the channel evenly with a fine to medium cut-flat hand file. The diamonds should be seated low enough that the walls can be filed together to ensure a parallel channel. If the diamonds are set too high to do this then file the tops of the channel walls separately and as little as needed to remove indentations.

Sometimes the metal must be slanted from the inner edges of the channel to the sides of the mounting. This is necessary when the metal is too thin

BASIC OPEN CHANNEL 77

to remove any more from directly above the diamonds. In such a case some smaller abrasions can remain to be removed later with emery paper. Whatever is done to one channel wall must also be done to the opposite wall. The symmetrics can be checked by looking at the channel from an end view.

STEP 18. Trim the metal at the inner edges on each channel wall along the crown facets of the diamonds. Use a NO. 6 barrette file, or three corner, needle file. File in a straight path to slightly bevel the metal from the diamonds. If a file cannot be used because the metal is too thin, or for any other reason, then use a NO. 40 flat graver with a polished tip to trim the metal (See Fig. 3.10). When completed, the metal on both sides of the channel should be formed identically (See Fig. 3.11). For that to happen more metal normally has to be removed from the undercut wall.

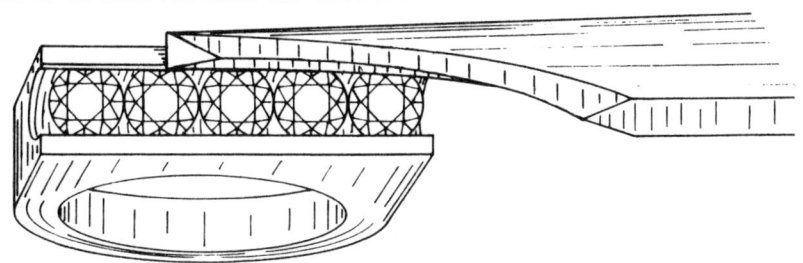

Fig. 3.10 Shows the small bevel of metal that extends over the diamonds being trimmed by a flat graver.

STEP 19. Smooth the inner edges of the channel walls. This can be done with a knife edge pumice wheel. Use the wheel in a brushing manner with long strokes. The pumice wheel should only be used enough to smooth the tiny bevels. Applying too much pressure in one area will flatten the metal.

STEP 20. Smooth the top surface of the channel walls. This was not done sooner because when trimming the metal along the diamonds the file or graver could slip and cut the surface. First use NO. 2 emery paper wrapped on an emery stick to remove rough file marks. Then either use NO. 4/0 polishing paper on an emery stick or a large rubber wheel that has a flat edge.

Fig. 3.11 The metal on both sides of the channel should be trimmed equally.

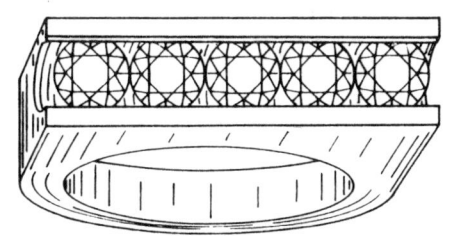

Fig. 3.12 Shows five diamonds channel set into a basic open channel.

STEP 21. Finish the sides of the mounting. Depending upon the degree of abrasions to the design, use a medium cut-flat hand file or NO. 2 emery paper. Removing deep indentations might be performed more easily by a coarser file or NO. 3 emery paper. In either case complete the finishing with NO. 2 emery paper followed by NO. 4/0 polishing paper. One final note is that when smoothing the metal keep the thickness and design equal on both sides of the channel.

3
Curved Channels

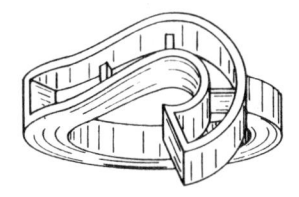

Circles, arcs, and other curvature shapes are useful in the design of unique jewelry. Channel setting diamonds into these contours is a little more complex than that of straight channels. Many of the same techniques are applicable although the use of some are restricted. One requirement is that the undercut bearings are cut into the outer curved wall of the channel. This is done because it is more practical to bend the metal from the inner arc to secure the diamonds towards the larger spanned wall. Gold will expand, but because of its mass it will not readily compress. That fact, coupled with the geometrics of the design, will cause an arch to resist movement towards a center point. Even if the channel is not undercut, the primary area of movement is still given to the inner curve to secure the diamonds. Other variations in the procedure include more intricate layout and finishing phases. The following steps describe how to channel set diamonds into a curve. The procedure can similarly be applied to more or less extravagant contours.

STEP 1. Inspect the mounting. Try to foresee problems that could develop because of the design, quality, and strength of the mounting. Examine the metal for pits and other possible casting defects. Check the structure of the undergallery and ring shank for support. These areas require a considerable amount of strength for some channel setting techniques. Curvature channels, such as the one being illustrated, typically have a channel extension beyond the direct support of the ring shank. Later in the procedure, measures should be taken to back up that section.

STEP 2. Inspect the diamonds. Look for inclusions and/or damage. Many flaws can be positioned in less conspicuous areas or in the channel bearing where they can be covered by the metal. In the illustrated example such diamonds may be set at the lower end of the channel. A damaged diamond should not be set unless the right person in authority is aware of it. Examine the characteristics of the diamonds that are to be set. Look for other things like thick or thin girdle facets that might require special attention later.

80 CURVED CHANNELS

STEP 3. Compare the channel dimensions and the diamonds. The width of the channel should be about three-fourths the diameter of the diamonds. If the walls need minor adjustment, use a combination flat/half round pliers to adjust the curved section and chain nose pliers for the straight section. The metal should be high enough from the finger area that the diamonds will not extend to the underside of the ring. Compare the channel length to be sure that all the diamonds will fit accordingly. A channel like the one being illustrated can be extended at the lower end by a cylinder bur then trimmed with a knife and flat graver.

STEP 4. Prepare the mounting for the layout. Examine the channel walls. They should both be the same height and thickness unless otherwise prescribed in the design. Some curved channels are intentionally slanted. File the tops of the channel walls together to be sure that they are parallel. Use long curving strokes following the contour of the channel. Afterwards emery the metal to remove file marks. Use a fine cut-flat hand file or barrette needle file, and NO. 2 emery paper.

STEP 5. Lay out the diamonds. Place all the diamonds table facets down on the channel to mark their locations. Bees wax might have to be applied to the metal to keep the diamonds stable. Position the diamonds to where there is an equal space between them, if any, and they are centered between the channel walls.

STEP 6. Mark the layout locations of the diamonds. Use a scriber or pointed graver to mark the metal between the diamonds to distinguish borders (See Fig. 4.2). One mark between the diamonds should be sufficient on the metal at the inner curve. The metal at the outer curve will have more open space between the diamonds. It might be necessary to engrave two border marks there—one for each diamond.

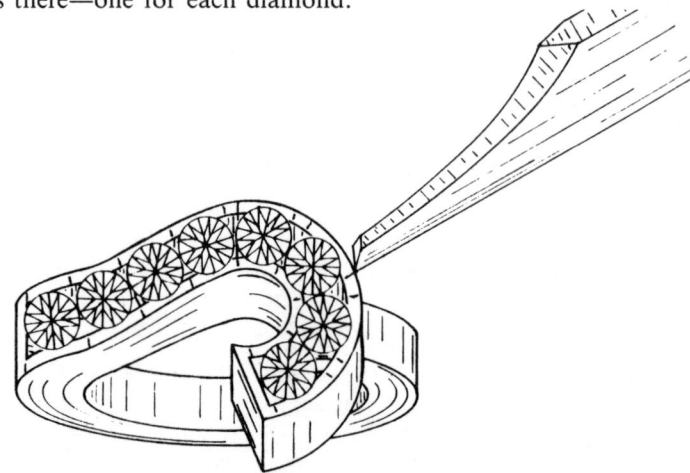

Fig. 4.2 Using a graver to mark the layout locations of the diamonds.

CURVED CHANNELS 81

STEP 7. Remove the diamonds from the layout. As each diamond is removed, place it in order in a diamond tray. Maintain that order throughout the channel setting procedure. One suggestion is to position the diamonds on the diamond tray in a curvature formation similar to the channel design (See Fig 4.3). This will help to keep the diamonds in order during the procedure when they are transferred repeatedly between the diamond tray and channel.

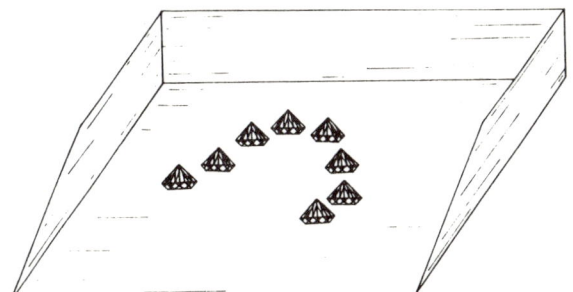

Fig. 4.3 Diamonds positioned in a curvature formation on a diamond tray so that the bearings can be cut specifically for each one without mixing them up.

STEP 8. Cut the bearings. In most curvature channels, and certainly this particular design, the bearings are undercut into the channel wall that has the larger arc. The diamonds are secured by bending the metal onto them from the channel wall that has the smaller arc. That will force the diamonds to be secured also by the undercut wall. It is more effective and efficient to secure diamonds from the center of a curve rather than from an outside curve. When metal is forced inward from an arc, it tends to buckle or spring back similar to that of pushing into a rubber ball.

To begin undercutting the bearings first make a test cut. The bearings should start at the top end of the channel as shown in figure 4.4 in case the channel unexpectedly has to be extended to contain the last diamond. In a channel such as the one illustrated there will be extra metal at the lower end to do this. Tilt the hart bur into the channel with the cutting edge of the bur at the bearing level. Place it against the wall that is to be undercut and centered between the border markings. The depth of the bearing should be one and one-half times the distance from the girdle of the diamond to its table facet. That will leave plenty of metal above the tables of the diamonds after they are seated to secure them and to finish later. After an initial cut is partially made into the metal, remove the bur to inspect the cut. It should be level, at the suggested bearing depth, and centered between the layout border markings. If not, adjust the position of the bur shaft.

Proceed to cut the bearings into the wall that is to be undercut. Try a few

82 CURVED CHANNELS

sizes of hart burs from smaller to larger to be sure that the bearings will not be too large. While undercutting one wall, gradually tilt the shaft of the bur upright to make a vertical cut down the opposite channel wall to the bearing level. Both cuts should be made simultaneously and to the same distance into each wall. Stop the vertical movement when the shaft of the bur is nearly perpendicular to the channel (See Fig. 4.4). This is a precaution to avoid cutting too much. As each bearing is completed, check to see if the diamond assigned there will fit, then place it back into the diamond tray. Do not cut more than a few bearings without testing the diamonds for overlapping, uniform depth, and other potential problems.

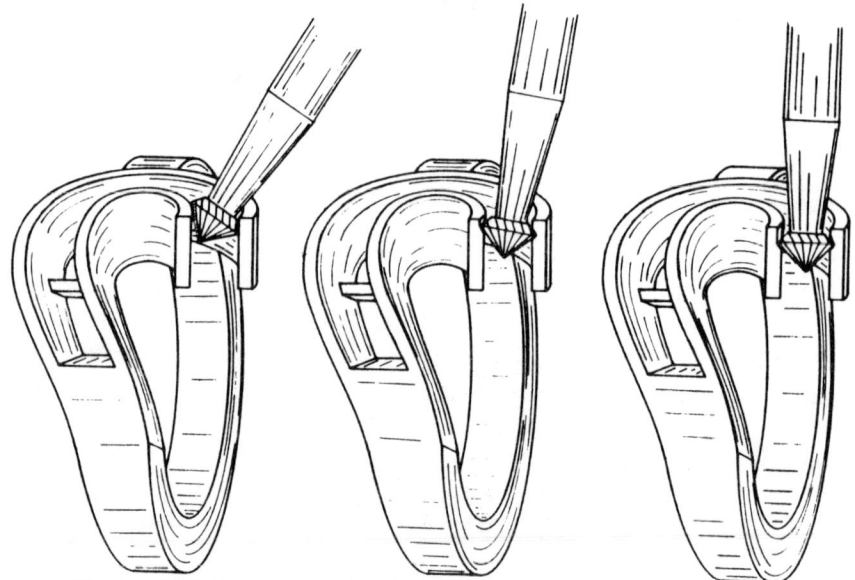

Fig. 4.4 Method to undercut bearings into a curved channel using a hart bur. Undercut into the outer arc wall of a curvature channel.

STEP 9. Clean the channel and diamonds. Brush the channel to remove loose metal and other debris from the bearings. Look directly into the bearings to be sure there are no obstructing metal particles. Clean the diamonds by rubbing them one at a time between a thumb and forefinger, or by tumbling them across a cloth via a finger tip.

STEP 10. Seat the diamonds. Replace the diamonds into the respective bearings by the order that they are in the diamond tray. Use bees wax tapered to a point to handle the diamonds by touching it to the table facets. Tilt each diamond into the undercut, then push down the opposite side via a fingernail or soft material such as a piece of wood.

STEP 11. Inspect the seating arrangement. The diamonds should be level, equally spaced, and to a uniform depth. Check for this from a side and end

CURVED CHANNELS 83

view of the channel. If adjustments are necessary that require re-cutting a bearing, then remove adjacent diamonds to avoid damaging them or the bur.

STEP 12. Secure the diamonds. Use slimline combination-half round/flat nose pliers to secure diamonds into a channel similar to the one being illustrated. For lack of room to position the pliers some circular channels have to be secured from the inner circular wall by tapping the metal (See Hammering/Tapping pg. 40). To use pliers brace the flat jaw flush against the outside of the undercut channel and the half round jaw against the edge of the opposite channel wall (See Fig. 4.5). Hold the mounting and pliers in a position that when the pliers are squeezed the metal can be seen bending onto the diamonds.

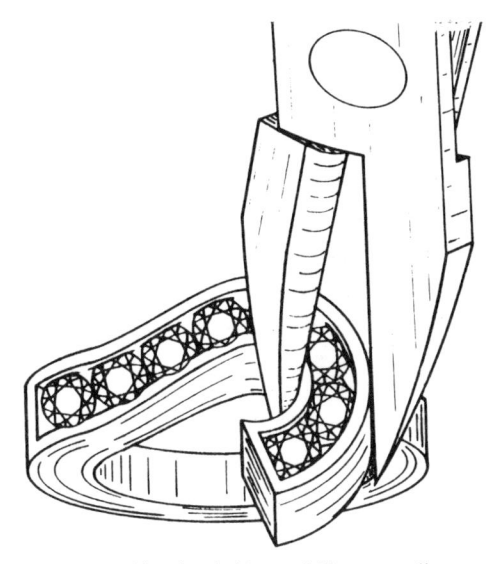

Fig. 4.5   Using combination half round/flat nose pliers to secure diamonds into an undercut curvature channel.

First bend the metal a little at each diamond along the channel to pre-tighten the diamonds. With each move watch for the effect that it has on the mounting and diamonds. After that, bend the metal at each diamond again and the metal between the diamonds. Shift the pliers along the channel stopping at each area to bend the metal. Eventually the entire top of the channel wall should be uniformly bent to secure the diamonds. Afterwards check the security of the undercut side by repeating the same technique to that side. Do not try to force the metal there to bend. It will not move as much except where a diamond is loosely seated.

If the wall at the inner arc will not bend easily, the metal can be burnished. One trick to do this is with the use of chain nose pliers (See Fig. 4.6). Hold the pliers at a low angle to the diamonds. Brace one jaw against the

84 CURVED CHANNELS

side of the undercut wall but considerably farther along the channel. Place the edge of the other plier jaw against the edge of the opposite channel wall. Squeeze the pliers firmly to force the jaw that is not braced to slide along the edge of the channel wall towards the opposite position of the other jaw. Repeat the process several times to burnish the metal onto the diamonds. Be careful not to flatten the metal or let the pliers slip.

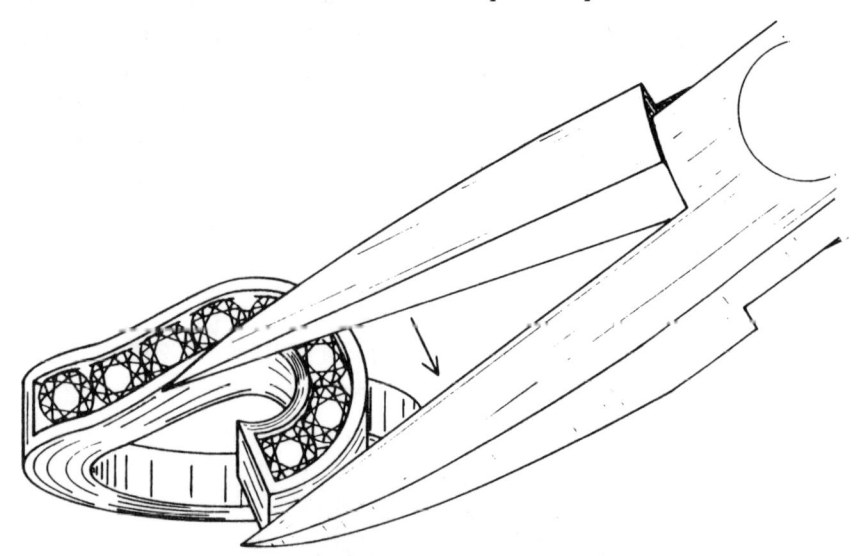

Fig. 4.6 Shows chain nose pliers positioned to burnish the inner arc wall of a curved channel onto the diamonds.

STEP 13. Close the gap between the top of the channel walls and the diamonds. The diamonds should be well secured at the girdles by the previous use of the pliers. However, that technique is limited as to how far the metal can be bent. Maneuvering pliers to bend the metal closer to the crown facets might require sacrificing the advantages of bracing one jaw flatly against one side of the channel. In effect the metal would probably become severely indented and/or the channel could collapse. Even worse, the diamonds could chip. Still, there is the gap to contend with that is distractive, and some doubt as to the future security of the diamonds. The recommended method to close the gap is by tapping the metal.

Normally the side that is not undercut is tapped first, then the undercut side. In this case of a curvature channel it is the innermost curve that is tapped first. If the undercuts are not properly made or any diamonds are tilting, then an exception will have to be made to reverse the order. The idea is that when tapping the metal onto a diamond it will not shift from the ledge in the undercut wall. Position the side of the channel that is being tapped in a fixture (mandrel, BenchMate™, padded vice, etc.) where the metal can be

CURVED CHANNELS 85

seen as it is moved toward the crown facets of the diamonds. If the diamonds extend into the finger area of the ring use a fixture that will not contact the diamonds. Also since this type of channel extends to the side, be sure that it is braced underneath by the fixture. If necessary pack the mounting with diamond setters cement so that the force of tapping will be absorbed by the fixture.

To tap the metal use a chasing hammer and a tapping tool that tapers to a flat-circular tip about one millimeter diameter. Hold the tapping tool to a position so that the metal is forced toward the crown facets rather than away from the diamonds (See Fig. 4.7). Hit the end of the tapping tool with the chasing hammer briskly and solid. Tap the metal a little at a time along the channel wall repeatedly. The metal could be seriously indented if it is tapped continuously in one area or with excessive force. It is not necessary nor advisable to tap the metal completely to the crown facets. Much of the overhanging edge will be trimmed back later regardless during the finishing phase.

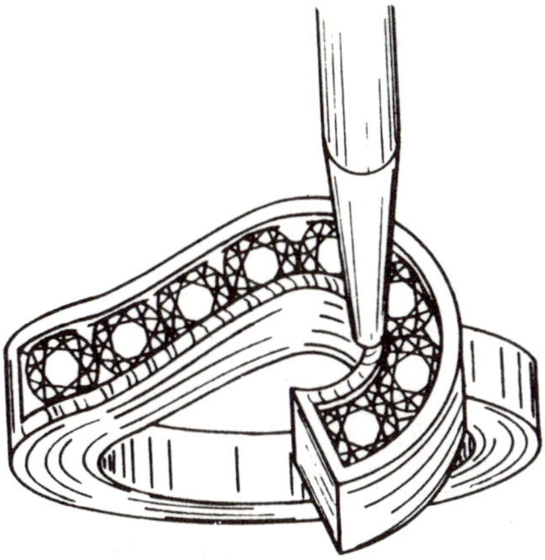

Fig. 4.7 Shows a tapping tool bending the channel metal closer to the diamonds.

STEP 14. Check the diamonds for security. The diamonds can be checked for tightness by gently pressing down on them at opposite sides with a pointed tool or by touching them with bees wax. Be careful when using any method other than bees wax because the diamonds can become loose or chipped. Loose diamonds usually result from bearings that are cut too large. If tightening is necessary, repeat STEP 12 to the loose diamond or tap the metal farther as discussed in the previous step.

STEP 15. File the metal on top of the channel walls to remove indentations. Use a fine cut-flat hand file or barette needle file. Try to file both walls of the channel together to keep them parallel. If the diamonds are seated too

86 CURVED CHANNELS

high, the channel walls will have to be filed separately. In either case they should be shaped to the original design.

STEP 16. File the sides of the mounting to remove indentations. The outer curve of a channel can be filed with a medium cut-flat hand file or barrette needle file. Use a medium cut-round or oval needle file to remove dents from the metal at the inside curves.

STEP 17. Emery the top and sides of the mounting to remove file marks. Use NO. 2 emery paper wrapped on an emery stick. The corners of the emery stick can sometimes be used at the inside curves. In hard to reach areas a rubber wheel might be helpful.

STEP 18. Trim the channel. Use a flat graver with a polished tip to trim the metal that extends over the diamonds (See Fig. 4.8). This metal is usually left irregular by the securing techniques. It should be trimmed uniformly on both sides of the channel. The metal will probably have to be beveled somewhat, but keep it as steep as possible.

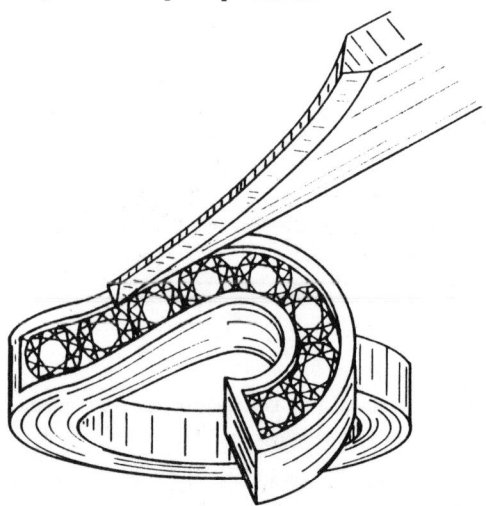

Fig. 4.8 Using a flat graver to trim the metal that extends onto the diamonds.

STEP 19. Trim the mounting. Remove sharp edges by lightly filing with appropriate shapes of needle files. Do not bevel the edges any more than what is absolutely necessary to refine the design.

STEP 20. Smooth the metal. Much of the metal can be smoothed by a large rubber wheel that has a flat edge. Spacious areas of metal should be smoothed by NO. 4/0 polishing paper wrapped on an emery stick. Smaller and hard to get areas may be smoothed with a knife edge pumice wheel.

4

Tapered Channels

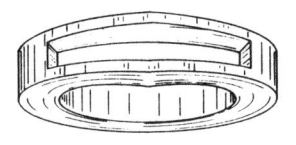

Tapered channels are typical in fashionable jewelry. The assembly procedure does not diverse too far from a basic channel setting. There are only a few exceptions. One significant difference is that various sizes of diamonds are intentionally used. With that being the case, the bearings are cut at various depths in order for the table facets of the diamonds to be positioned on a uniform plane. Another transition from a basic channel setting procedure is that the bearings in a tapered channel are not equally spaced as in channels that have equal sized diamonds. Likewise, the distance between the diamonds are proportionately spaced. As compared to more basic types, tapered channels involve additional tool changing and increased concentration to setting diamonds in perspective to the sum of the diamonds.

STEP 1. Inspect the mounting. First check the design to see that it is suitable for channel setting. The channel discussed and illustrated in this procedure is tapered. A mounting may include a tapered section along with other shapes or consist of only a taper. In either event the channel walls should compliment each other to form a symmetric design.

Examine the metal for defects and weaknesses that could affect the procedure. If any part of a channel wall is imperfect, it will influence the whole channel. There is no point to attempt making corrections until all aspects of the mounting and diamonds are inspected. After every feature is considered, a better decision can be made as to what action to take. In most cases only precautionary measures are necessary.

STEP 2. Inspect the diamonds. Make a note of particular diamonds that will require special treatment later. Diamonds that have thick girdle facets require deeper bearings so the table facets will not set too high. Those with thin girdle facets or certain types of flaws will chip easier. Also, lower quality diamonds and smaller sizes should be set in a manner or position where they will be less distracting. Both natural and unnatural imperfections will have a direct effect on certain phases of the procedure and ultimately the outcome.

88 TAPERED CHANNELS

STEP 3. Recut the channel if necessary. A tapered channel usually requires some adjustment. The most common problem is that the length is not opened far enough, but like all channels the width also might be too wide or too narrow. To check the channel dimensions, first file the top to be sure both walls are even and there are no depressions. Use a fine cut-flat hand file or a barrette needle file, whichever is more suitable. Then place the diamonds table facets down in a tapered order across the channel. Position the diamonds centered both lengthwise and between the walls. With the diamonds spaced as they will be set, the channel dimensions can then be analyzed. If the length is too short, use a scriber or pointed graver to mark cutting borders on the metal, then remove the diamonds.

Adjusting the length of the channel can first be done by a tapered cylinder bur if much metal has to be removed. This type of bur is ideal to extend tapered channels. By using it the end of the channel can gradually be cut narrower by raising the bur more and more as the cutting approaches to the desired length. After the bulk of metal has been removed to the end border marks the metal might have to be trimmed. Only a knife or anglette graver is necessary if the taper is to be cut to a point. If the design calls for the ends to be squared, use a knife graver to cut the corners then use a flat graver or square needle file to shape the metal.

The width of the channel at each area where a diamond will be set should be about three-fourths the diameter of the diamond at that location. Widening and narrowing a tapered channel can usually be done by flat nose pliers. Depend upon a flat graver to complete the trimming inside the channel.

STEP 4. Pre-finish the channel metal. The metal in a channel that has been altered will likely be rough, to some degree, wherever it has been cut. In order to make precise judgments throughout the remaining phases of the procedure, the channel should be free of abrasions. First use NO. 2 emery paper wrapped on an emery stick to remove file marks and other obstructions from the top of the channel walls. This will allow layout markings to be clearly recognized. Smooth the walls in the channel with a knife edge pumice wheel as much as possible without distorting the edges of the channel walls. If it is feasible, pre-polish the channel. Once the diamonds have been secured, this area cannot be finished easily.

STEP 5. Arrange the diamonds in a tapered order on a diamond tray. Position the diamonds in line and table facets down on the tray. From a top view shift the diamonds until an equal taper can be formed at each end of the line. Place higher quality diamonds nearer the center if differences in size is not compromised. Also, distribute lower quality diamonds equally at both ends. In other words, do not put all the better or worse diamonds at one end of the tapered line.

TAPERED CHANNELS 89

STEP 6. Mark one end of the diamond tray and one end of the channel. This is done to keep the diamonds in order when they are transferred repeatedly from the tray to the mounting for test fitting while the bearings are being cut. A diamond's serial order in a taper is not easily misinterpreted, but the bearings are not always equal for respective diamonds at opposite ends of the taper. When a bearing is cut at one end of the channel for a particular diamond, then that diamond should be assured of being seated into that bearing—not in the corresponding bearing at the other end of the channel. By marking the channel L-(left) and R-(right) then whenever a technique is performed to the mounting it is held in that position to keep the diamonds in their respective order.

STEP 7. Lay out the diamonds. First adjust dividers by trial and error from each end of the channel until a common distance can be found to denote the center. Engrave two tick marks at that point—one on each side of the channel (See Fig. 5.2). Then lay out the diamonds table facets down and equally spaced from the center diamond (or between the two center diamonds if applicable) on that position. Spreading a film of bees wax on the metal will help to keep the diamonds stable.

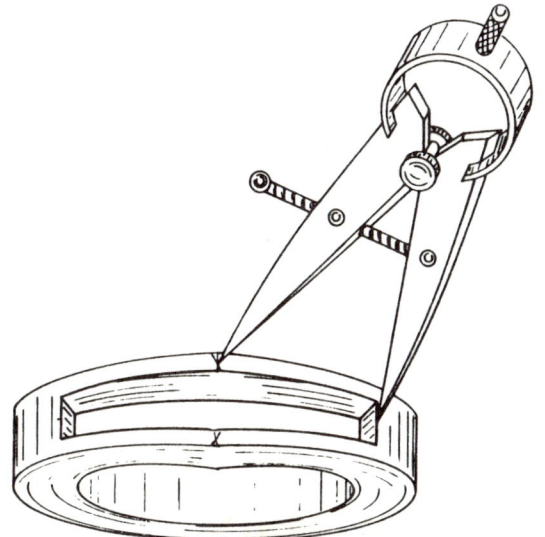

Fig. 5.2 Find the center of a straight tapered channel by adjusting dividers by trial and error from the ends.

STEP 8. Mark the layout location of each diamond. The marks will be used as guides when the bearings are being cut. A tick mark more like a scratch between the diamonds and at both ends on each side of the channel should be sufficient (See Fig. 5.3). Use a scriber or a pointed graver but do not cut deep into the metal.

90 TAPERED CHANNELS

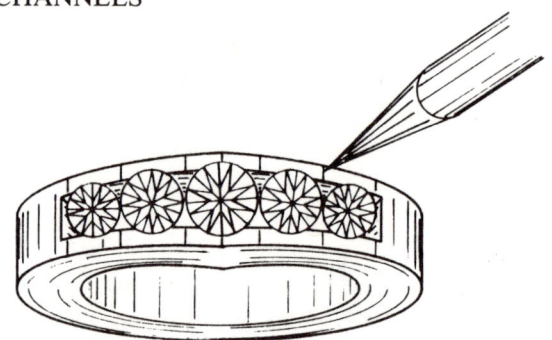

Fig. 5.3 Shows diamonds laid out table facets down on a tapered channel. A scriber is used to mark the layout.

STEP 9. Remove the diamonds. Be sure to place the diamonds back on the diamond tray in the same order as before. Refer to the left-right marks designated on the mounting and diamond tray that were made in STEP 6. As each diamond is removed, make sure that it is clean by rubbing it between a thumb and finger tip. Stubborn wax particles can be removed by tumbling the diamonds via a finger tip on a bench cloth stretched over a flat surface. After all the diamonds are cleaned and replaced in the diamond tray, wipe the bees wax off of the channel if it was applied.

STEP 10. Cut the bearings. Hart burs are used because the bearing on one side of the channel will be undercut. Since the channel is to be tapered with diamonds, various sizes of burs will be used. Furthermore, it is safer to intentionally cut the bearings too small at first then gradually as needed to avoid over-cutting. This will require the use of even more burs. As each bearing is cut check to see that the diamond for that bearing will fit then replace it into its order in the diamond tray.

Mark the channel wall that will be undercut as a reminder or refer to the left-right position as discussed earlier. It is easy to become distracted during the procedure and forget which side is being undercut. If both sides of the channel are undercut at different locations, the bearing depth would be less controllable, as well as the securing technique to come. Either side can be undercut because the channel is straight, but it should be only one side.

Begin cutting the bearing for the center diamond and progress toward both ends. Each bearing should be cut centered between the layout marks. Tilt the bur into the side of the channel that is to be undercut with the shaft on a vertical axis in perspective to the channel. If the bur shaft is not positioned as described, the bearings will not be level. The cutting edge of the bur should be positioned at a level that is about one and one-half times the distance from the girdle of the diamond to be set there to the height of its table facet. As a result the smaller diamonds will be seated slightly higher than the larger ones, but their table facets will be on an equal plane across the channel.

Undercut into the metal to a point where the same distance can be cut into the opposite wall. At the same time pivot the bur from the undercut by straightening the bur shaft to cut vertically down the opposite channel wall (See Fig. 5.4). The power will have to be accelerated to medium speeds to cut both sides of the channel. When the bur shaft is nearly perpendicular to the channel, release the power. If the diamond will not set level, then reinsert the bur and cut to a more perpendicular position of the shaft. As each bearing is cut, test the seating arrangement for the diamond and compare it to the adjacent bearing. The diamonds will have to be removed and replaced occasionally to check for spacing and depth. A bearing should not be cut next to one that has a diamond seated in it.

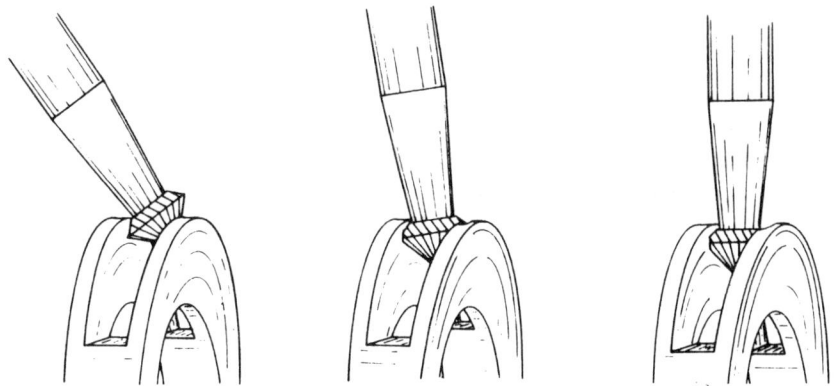

Fig. 5.4 Method to undercut one side of a tapered channel with a hart bur while simultaneously cutting a vertical bearing into the opposite wall.

STEP 11. Clean the channel and diamonds. The smallest particle of debris can affect seating a diamond. Brush the channel to remove metal shavings and other loose debris from the bearings. Clean the diamonds again by tumbling them across a cloth stretched over a flat surface or by rubbing them between a thumb and finger tip. Work with only one diamond at a time, then replace it back into the correct order in the diamond tray.

STEP 12. Seat the diamonds. Place all of the diamonds back into their bearings. They should be equally spaced with the table facets on an equal plane across the channel. If there are any inconsistencies such as unlevel diamonds or unequal spacing, then make the corrections now. Adjustments cannot be done as easily after the diamonds are secured.

STEP 13. Secure the diamonds. The diamonds are secured by bending the metal over the girdle facets from the side of the channel that is not undercut. The pressure on the diamonds from that side will also force the diamonds tight into the undercut metal. This can be done by pressing the metal with

92 TAPERED CHANNELS

pliers or by tapping. Pressing the metal is usually recommended especially in such a case as this where pliers can be manipulated on both sides of the mounting. By using pliers the diamonds are more likely to remain in position without bouncing about, and it is easier to control the metal movement because of the leverage factor. However, some degree of tapping is often necessary after the diamonds are secured to bend the channel metal closer to the crown facets of the diamonds. This is an option that is sometimes eliminated or applied in part at the discretion of the diamond setter.

Securing channel set diamonds by pliers can damage a mounting if the pliers are not used skillfully, or by using the wrong type. Slimline-chain nose pliers are required for this procedure. The size will limit the force although they are still capable of excessive pressure. By being small the visibility is less obstructed and the flat inner face of the jaws minimize distortion to the metal.

The technique to channel set diamonds by pliers is to brace one side of the channel with one jaw of the pliers while applying pressure to the upper edge of the opposite side. When securing the diamonds, first bend the upper portion of the channel wall that is not undercut. To do this brace the undercut side by placing one jaw of the pliers flatly against it. The other jaw should be placed against the outer edge of the opposite wall (See Fig. 5.5). Then squeeze the pliers at alternate locations along the channel to bend the metal over the girdles of the diamonds.

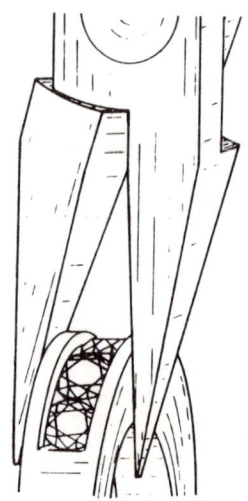

Fig. 5.5 Using chain nose pliers to secure diamonds into a tapered channel. Brace the undercut channel wall by placing one plier jaw flatly against it, then bend the upper metal from the opposite wall onto the diamond.

When securing the diamonds, do not bend any section of the channel completely over with one movement. Bend the metal a little at each diamond along the channel, then bend the metal between the diamonds. Repeat that technique several times until the diamonds are tight and the channel wall is folded evenly. Do not attempt to close the metal onto the crown facets with the pliers. That will usually require that the pliers be placed in a position that will severely distort the mounting. The girdle coverage should be sufficient. During the process continually watch the metal as it moves and check the positions of the diamonds. Afterwards, using less pressure, perform the same technique to the undercut side of the channel to ensure that the diamonds are tight.

STEP 14. Tap the metal closer to the crown facets of the diamonds. The urgency to do this depends upon how much metal was moved by the pliers and the security of the diamonds. The metal does not have to be completely pressed to the crown facets of the diamonds because they are secured at the girdles. Much of the metal is trimmed back later when the channel is finished. If any of the diamonds are still loose, or a large distractive gap exists, then tapping the metal might be necessary.

To tap the metal, first stabilize the ring on a sturdy fixture. If a mandrel is used, be sure that the diamonds do not protrude through the underside of the ring to it. Other fixtures that can be used include a BenchMate™, padded vice, and an engraving block. The non-undercut metal is tapped first. That side should be positioned where the metal can be seen as it closes toward the diamonds. Place the tip of the tapping tool flat against the metal with the shaft perpendicular or slightly towards the channel (See Fig. 5.6). Use a tapping tool that tapers to a flat circular tip about one millimeter diameter, and a lightweight chasing hammer.

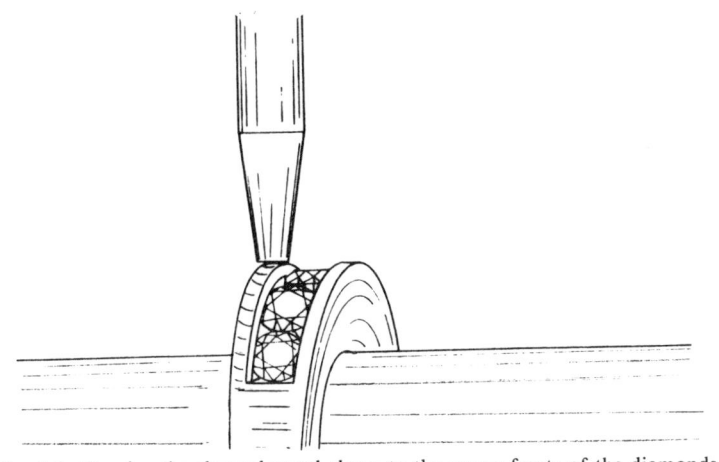

Fig. 5.6 Tapping the channel metal closer to the crown facets of the diamonds.

Tap the end of the tapping tool at a steady pace, while continually moving the tip along the channel wall. It is better to repeat the process several

94 TAPERED CHANNELS

times rather than concentrate on one area. Do not beat the metal hard or flush to the crown facets. That will either cause a diamond to chip or severely indent the metal. After the metal has been moved close to the crown facets, reverse the ring on the fixture to tap the undercut side of the channel. That side will not require as much movement because it is pre-formed over the diamonds. To conclude, tap the metal on both sides of the channel wherever necessary to smooth the indentations as much as possible.

STEP 15. Inspect the diamonds and mounting. Any adjustments to the mounting should be done before continuing to the finishing phase. Because of excessive or improper tapping, the diamonds could become loose or out of position. Likewise, the mounting might become distorted. Alterations of any type are serious at this stage, but it is better to discover the problems now rather than after the metal has been finished.

STEP 16. Remove indentations. The first task of the finishing phase is to file the metal to remove indentations caused by the pliers and tapping techniques. Use a medium cut-flat hand file for large areas and a barrette needle file for smaller areas. The objective is to re-shape the metal to its intended design. Do not remove any more metal than what is necessary. After filing use NO. 2 emery paper wrapped on an emery stick to remove the file marks. Emery paper can be used without filing if the indentations are not too deep.

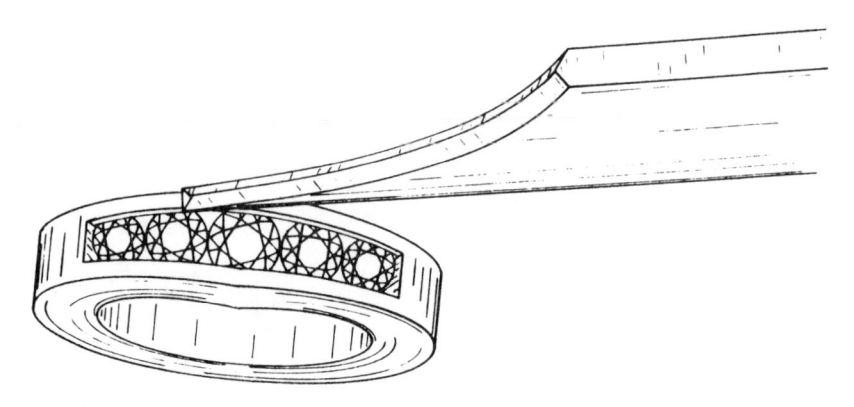

Fig. 5.7   Shows a flat graver trimming the metal that extends over the diamonds.

STEP 17. Trim the channel. Bevel the channel metal from the crown facets of the diamonds to the inner edge at the top of the channel walls. This metal that extends over the diamonds is usually rough and uneven. It should become uniform and equal on both sides of the channel. The diamonds should not be covered by more metal on one side of the channel. Since this is a tapered

TAPERED CHANNELS 95

channel most of the work will have to be done by a flat graver (See Fig. 5.7). Do not chop the metal. Use long shaving strokes. Try to cut the metal as steep as possible for a more attractive channel effect.

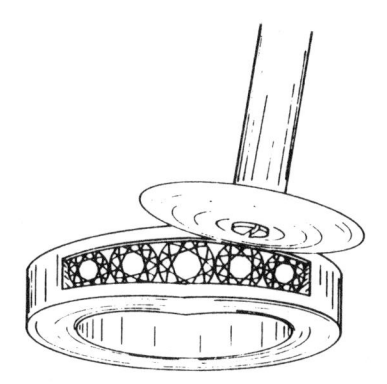

Fig. 5.8 Using a knife edge pumice wheel to smooth the bevel of metal that extends onto the diamonds.

STEP 18. Smooth the metal. Use a knife edge pumice wheel to lightly brush the bevel along the diamonds (See Fig. 5.8). Be careful because the metal can become disfigured if it is rubbed too much. The top and sides of the channel can become smooth similarly by a large rubber wheel that has a flat edge. Larger flat areas should be smoothed by NO. 4/0 polishing paper wrapped on an emery stick.

5

Angular Channels

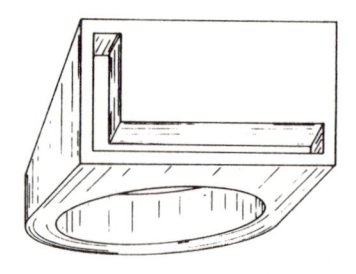

Setting diamonds into an angular channel could be a simple elaboration of a straight channel. Instead of one row there are two that extend from a corner forming a right angle. Thus, attention to the corner might be the only real difference. To compound what would otherwise be a fundamental task, this section describes the procedure to secure diamonds into an angular channel by more involved techniques. Previous illustrations have shown the diamonds being secured primarily by pliers with some inclusion of tapping the metal. Now an angular channel is presented as being the perimeter of a more massive area of metal. Using pliers to secure diamonds into this particular mounting would be awkward so the emphasis of the instruction is to "hammer set" the diamonds. Other discussions include the importance to setting diamonds low into a channel and its related purpose of finishing large areas of metal.

STEP 1. Inspect the mounting. Upon receipt of a large mounting like the one illustrated, there is reason to be suspicious. First of all, the consistency of smoothness during casting processes is less likely over wide areas of metal. Check the metal for shale and incomplete cavities. Second, large mountings are seldom solid. They can be assembled to appear whole. Check for solder seams. And third, long spans are flexible. A channel needs support to absorb pressure from channel setting techniques. Techniques can be adapted to compensate for imperfections in a mounting if the imperfections are detected early in the procedure.

STEP 2. Inspect the diamonds. Check for both natural and unnatural imperfections. Become familiar with the characteristics. This knowledge will be appreciated later in the procedure. For instance, the cut of the diamonds

ANGULAR CHANNELS 97

will influence the techniques to cut bearings and to secure the diamonds. Diamonds can be strategically positioned to expose favorable qualities and partially conceal undesirable features. Also, authorities are not always aware that a diamond is damaged. A diamond setter should never assume that all the defects in a selected group of diamonds are known by the employer or customer.

STEP 3. File the sides of the mounting. Use a fine to medium cut-flat hand file. This is done routinely to this type of mounting to ensure that the sides are straight, especially at the channel's outer walls. Do not file the channel walls too thin. Keep in mind that more metal will be removed from it during the finishing phase. For now be concerned about having a straight wall to set the diamonds.

STEP 4. File the top of the channel to be sure that the metal is planed. Begin this procedure with a flat surface rather than trying to correct it after the diamonds are set. Use a flat hand file to apply a cross filing technique until the file marks cover the surface by one pass. Cross filing is to file in one direction then file 45°-90° to the resulting file marks. A coarser cut-flat hand file may be used at first, followed by a finer cut.

STEP 5. Prepare the channel. The channel should have straight dimensions to a reasonable depth and width. Most alterations for a pre-cut channel can be done with a flat graver, knife, or anglette graver. If there is a basin, it should be flat and to a depth that is at least twice the distance from the girdles of the diamonds to the height of the table facets. At this depth the diamonds can be seated well below the surface of the channel with the girdles above the basin. If there are any holes in the basin, they should be complete and equal in diameter.

The width of the channel should be about three-fourths the diameter of the diamonds. That will leave an ample amount of metal to cut a bearing into each side of the channel. This distance can be roughly checked by comparing the diamond(s) to the channel. The width is too large if the diamond will not set over the channel without falling into it. Conversely, the channel width is too narrow if the diamond cannot be tilted into the channel towards one wall (at any angle) because the culet is blocked by the opposite wall. Be sure that the walls of the channel are straight from corner to corner and perpendicular. Use a flat graver to cut the side walls, and use a knife or anglette graver to sharpen the corners.

STEP 6. Lay out the diamonds. Space the diamonds table facets down on the channel. Apply bees wax on the metal to temporarily stabilize them. Place one diamond squared in the corner to define the angle. If there is a size variation among the diamonds, select the largest one for the corner.

98 ANGULAR CHANNELS

Space the others in line and equally to the ends. Leave the same distance between the end diamonds and the ends of the channel. This should be done even if the spacing between the two rows is different.

STEP 7. Mark the layout locations of the diamonds. These inscriptions will serve as a guide for accurate spacing when the bearings are cut. Use a scriber or pointed graver to mark the borders between diamonds and at the ends of both sides of the channel (See Fig. 6.2). Do not cut deep into the metal. Tiny scratches about one-half millimeter long should be sufficient to denote the borders. The marks can be extended later. To attempt it now with the diamonds intact could cause them to shift.

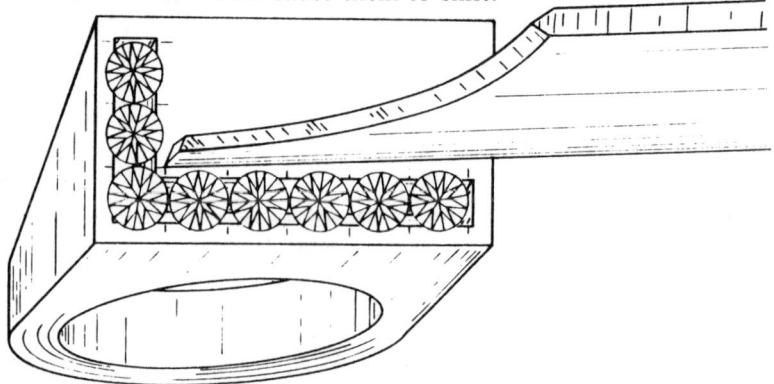

Fig. 6.2 Using a pointed graver to mark the layout locations of diamonds on an angular channel.

STEP 8. Remove the diamonds from the layout and place them in the same angular formation on a diamond tray. As each diamond is removed, clean and position it in the respective order on the tray. Afterwards, wipe the bees wax from the metal if it was applied and brush the channel.

STEP 9. Inspect the layout marks to make specific notations. While the layout positions of the diamonds are fresh in mind, continue and clarify the marks. Without them some important details decided during this phase might be overlooked later when other phases of the procedure will depend upon these references.

STEP 10. Cut the bearings. Use a hart bur to undercut the metal at the inner channel wall and vertical cut the bearing into the outer wall. That will allow the diamonds to be secured by bending the metal from the outer channel wall. The outer wall in this case is easier to manipulate. Graduate the sizes of hart burs used to cut the bearings from smaller to larger to avoid cutting them too large. Because of vibration under power, a bur that appears to be the right size could cut a much larger bearing than its diameter.

Make a test cut to see if the hart bur is positioned correctly to cut the bearings level and at the right depth. Tilt the bur into the channel from the

ANGULAR CHANNELS 99

perimeter of the mounting to place the cutting edge between border markings at the proposed bearing depth (See Fig. 6.3A). This is about one and one-half times the distance between the girdle of the diamond to the height of its table facet. A diamond secured at that depth should set as recommended with its table facet just below the surface of the mounting. Start the bur cutting slowly until it begins to cut steadily into the metal under control and without struggling. Then remove the bur to examine the beginning of the bearing. It should be between the guidelines at the right depth and level. Otherwise, re-position the bur to make adjustments.

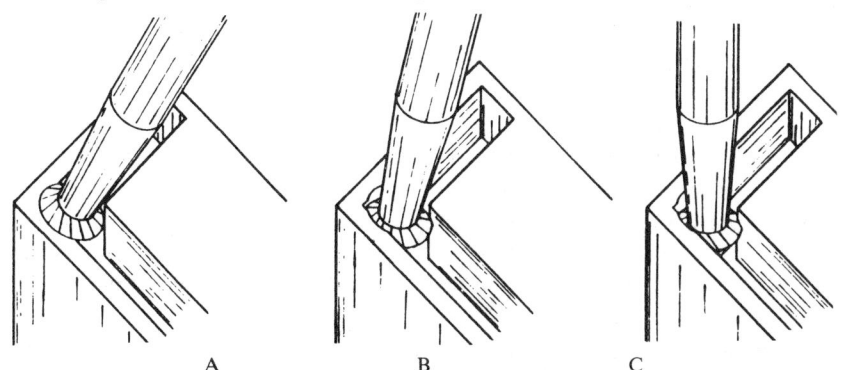

Fig. 6.3 Method to undercut bearings into an angular channel using a hart bur. Begin at the corner bearing.

Cut the corner bearing first, then progress toward the ends. The bearings are undercut and vertically cut simultaneously (See Fig. 6.3B&C). To do this tilt the bur back while undercutting into the inner channel wall until the shaft is nearly perpendicular to the channel. Eventually the same distance should be cut into both channel walls although the perimeter walls are cut vertically to the bearing (See Fig. 6.4). Do not straighten the bur shaft completely. If the bearing happens to be cut too large, the diamond will be set unlevel when it is secured. It is safer to recut the bearing later as needed. A bearing that is cut too high or unlevel into this type of channel could be disastrous to the procedure because corrections are troublesome at this area.

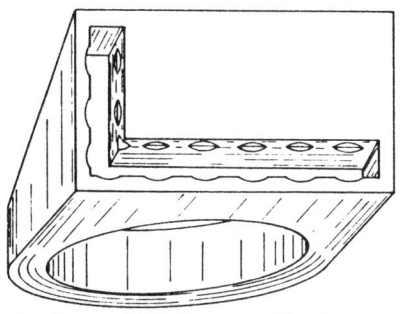

Fig. 6.4 Shows bearings undercut into one side of an angular channel and vertical cut into the opposite side.

100 ANGULAR CHANNELS

STEP 11. Seat the diamonds. As each bearing is cut check it to see how the diamond assigned for that bearing fits. Recut the metal as necessary with the diamond out. When the diamond fits properly, place it back in order on the diamond tray. Continue to cut the remaining bearings by a similar routine. After all the bearings are cut, brush the channel and clean the diamonds then seat them permanently.

STEP 12. Inspect the seating arrangement. The diamonds should be level and equally spaced; however, it is not unusual that the spacing of the diamonds differ between each of the two adjoining channels. Also, the diamonds for either the side or end extension of the angular channel should be left out until the other is secured. Otherwise, the diamonds will likely be jarred loose while the adjoining channel is being secured.

STEP 13. Secure the diamonds. The diamonds are secured into this particular channel by hammer setting. A mandrel is used as a fixture to hold the ring in the illustrations, but a BenchMate™, padded vice, or engraving block could also be used. Metal from the outside perimeter wall is bent to secure the diamonds via a tapping tool and chasing hammer. The procedure, as discussed here, focuses on securing the side extension of the angular channel first, although the order may be reversed. The technique to follow is tedious and lengthy. Take time, and occasionally stop to relax and check the work.

Place the ring on the mandrel with the side of the mounting to be hammered farthest from view (See Fig. 6.5). In other words the undercut side of the channel is closest to the craftsman and the wider end of the mandrel. From that view, the effects of tapping can be seen, and the hammering is less likely to force the ring loose on the mandrel. Be sure that the diamonds do not extend through the underside of the ring to the fixture. If so, then the ring will have to be secured in an alternate fixture. If all is well, pull the ring tightly on the mandrel.

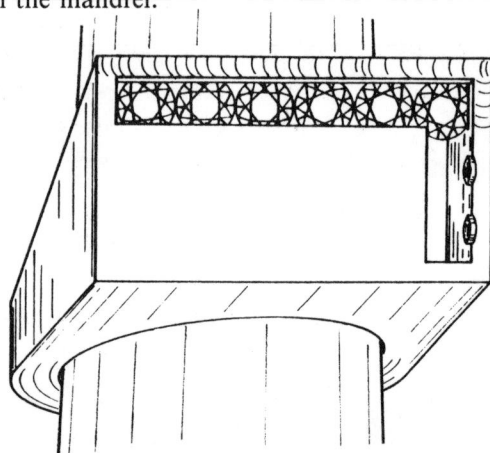

Fig. 6.5 Shows the position of an angular channel on a mandrel to view the metal as it is tapped onto the diamonds. Notice that only one extension of the channel is tapped at a time although all the bearings are pre-cut.

ANGULAR CHANNELS 101

If the diamonds are not seated snug because of poorly cut bearings, they will vibrate in the channel when the metal is tapped. To compensate, the diamonds may be semi-secured one at a time until a normal tapping technique can be performed. To pre-tighten the diamonds, hold them down by a finger or narrow graver. Tap the outer channel metal lightly at about 45° with the ball head of the chasing hammer. If a graver is used to hold the diamonds down, keep it out of the direct path of the hammer. The objective here is to hammer just enough to keep the diamonds stable, not to secure them.

To secure the diamonds permanently use a tapping tool that has a flat circular tip about one millimeter in diameter. A shorter tip could cause excessive indentation. A wider tip will obstruct the view and possibly require too much force to bend the metal. The metal should be seen moving as it is tapped. Begin tapping along the upper edge of the channel's outer wall at about 45° towards the diamonds (See Fig. 6.6A). This will move the metal tight to the girdles of the diamonds and cause it to bend partially over the channel. Do not tap continuously in one area. That could seriously indent the metal or cause a diamond to chip. Keep the tapping tool moving along the metal. Furthermore, tap the end of the tool squarely with the chasing hammer at a rhythmic speed.

Fig. 6.6 Shows hammering/tapping the perimeter of an angular channel wall to secure a diamond.

When the metal is bent over the girdles of the diamonds, the tapping tool can be tilted to a higher angle. Tapping the metal from that direction will cause the metal to bend closer to the crown facets of the diamonds (See Fig. 6.6B). Use the same method as before to keep the tapping tool moving, and hammer at a steady pace.

The extreme ends of the channel do not require hammering. Both sides of the corner diamond must be hammered from the outside channel wall but not necessarily the inside corner metal. If the diamonds are still loose after hammering the outside channel wall, then reluctantly the inside channel wall must be hammered also. The procedures should involve this metal as little as possible because it is more troublesome to finish.

To hammer the inside channel wall, the tapping tool is held upright to

102 ANGULAR CHANNELS

the metal. More importantly the tip of the tool should be a little wider in diameter and kept just within the edge of the metal (See Fig. 6.7). In this manner the metal cannot become as seriously indented or beveled to the diamonds. The metal will have to move towards the diamonds because it is the natural direction rather than toward the bulk of metal in the center area of the mounting. Even if the tapping tool is directed slightly away from the diamonds, the metal being pliable as it is will be apt to move towards the diamonds since its movement is restricted by the mass of metal.

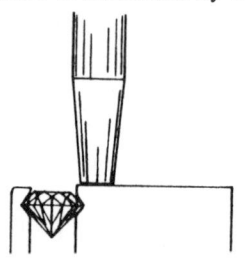

Fig. 6.7 When it is necessary to tap metal onto diamonds from a wide area try to keep the tapping tool within the edge of the channel to avoid beveling the metal.

Hammer setting the channel at the end of the mounting is similar to the side channel. One difference is that when a mandrel is used, the tapping tool has to be tilted slightly in a direction that will force the mounting towards the wide end of the mandrel. Slanting the tapping tool to either end of a channel is contrary to basic instruction, but in this situation it is an exception. Otherwise, the hammering thrust will cause the mounting to slip on the mandrel. The only recourse is to use one of the clamping fixtures.

STEP 14. Remove indentations. Use a medium cut-flat hand file to file the top and sides of the mounting. Be careful not to file the metal too thin. More metal will be removed afterwards when the metal is emeried to remove file marks. Some dents from hammering might be so deep that an excessive amount of metal would have to be filed. Use the tapping technique to smooth the largest dents.

STEP 15. Remove file marks. Use NO. 2 emery paper wrapped on an emery stick. Do not emery too much. There will be a tendency for the edges of the mounting to become rounded. If a lot of emerying is necessary, place the mounting on a flat surface to draw it back and forth using the fingers to push it flat.

STEP 16. Trim the channel. Use a flat graver that has a polished tip to trim the metal that extends over both sides of the channel. It is favorable for design purposes to bevel the metal steep from the crown facets of the diamonds to the surface of the plate. The outside edges of the channel might have to

ANGULAR CHANNELS 103

be slightly beveled also to straighten the design. This can be done with a NO. 6 barrette needle file.

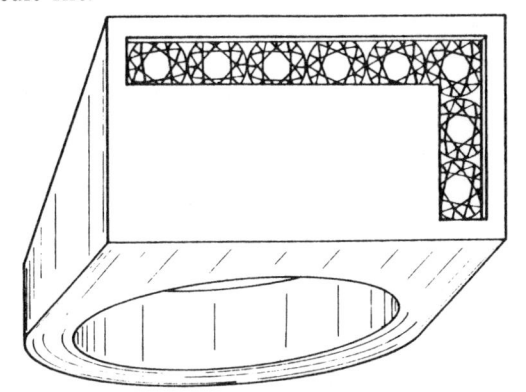

FIg. 6.8 Shows eight diamonds set into an angular channel.

STEP 17. Smooth the metal. The abrasive emeried surfaces can become smooth by using NO. 4/0 polishing paper wrapped on an emery stick. Smooth the metal wherever emery paper was used. If the beveled metal in the channel from the diamonds to the surface of the plate are choppy or rough, use a knife edge pumice wheel to smooth it.

6

Inlaid Channels (Round Diamonds)

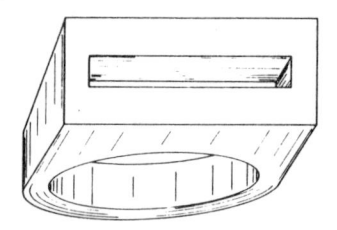

An inlaid channel is one that is centered within a large mass of metal. There are no narrow walls that can be simply "bent" to secure the diamonds. Setting diamonds into an inlaid channel is a higher echelon of diamond setting. It is an extreme variation of basic channel setting. To successfully complete the procedure requires proficiency in every phase of channel setting. There is hardly an acceptable tolerance from beginning to end. If there is a unique learning experience to be derived from this procedure it is to take time, relax, and occasionally stop to inspect the work and plan each subsequent move.

STEP 1. Inspect the mounting. First check to see that the channel is not too wide. An inlaid channel can be widened, but it might not be practical to make it narrower. Any adjustments that are feasible may be done later. For now, before going any farther, place one of the diamonds on top of the channel to be sure the procedure can continue.

Other factors to be concerned about at this time are the strength of the mounting and impurities in the metal that could hamper the craftsmanship. Defects in the mounting are not always serious enough to stop the procedure, but they usually require at least a mental note that the problems do exist.

STEP 2. Examine the diamonds. Use an eye loupe to search for chips, flaws and other imperfections. All the diamonds should be the same quality, and in this case, the same size. It is discouraging to perform skillful work only to have it rejected because of the previous condition of the diamonds. Try to solve these inadequacies before setting the diamonds. Inform authoritative personnel if there is any doubt about the diamonds.

STEP 3. Compare the channel and diamonds. Inspect the width, depth, and length of the channel. An ideal width for most channels is about three-fourths the diameter of the diamonds. For an inlaid channel the width should be a little more so that a minimal amount of damage is done to the surface

INLAID CHANNELS (ROUND DIAMONDS) 105

when the bearings are cut. The metal of inlaid channels cannot be manipulated as well as channels having narrow walls. Still, the diamonds should be set on top of the channel without falling into it. The depth of a channel is the distance from the surface of the channel to the basin, or in this example, the finger area of the ring. The diamonds should eventually be seated with the table facets just below the surface and the culets not extended into the finger area. Compare the depth to the diamonds by placing one diamond to the side of the channel. To check the length, place the diamonds girdle to girdle on the channel.

STEP 4. Prepare the channel. An inlaid channel usually requires some adjustment because it is made for various sizes of diamonds. If it is nearly the correct size, the alterations can be completed with a knife or anglette graver, and a flat graver. Otherwise, a series of burs, such as a cylinder and wheel bur, may be used first. To trim the channel, cut the corners with a knife or anglette graver, then use a flat graver to plane the dimensions to the corners. Also, cross file the top of the mounting. It is important that the procedure begins with the top surface having no depressions nor elevations. First file in one direction with a medium cut-flat hand file until the entire surface is covered with file marks by one pass. Then file 45°-90° to those file marks in a similar manner.

STEP 5. Remove file marks. This is done so that layout markings will not be confused with file marks. Emery the surface with NO. 2 emery paper wrapped on an emery stick. Do not emery any more metal than necessary to remove the file marks. The metal will be filed and emeried again later. As mentioned, it is done now only to ensure that the procedure begins from a planed surface, and the layout marks to follow will be clear.

STEP 6. Lay out the diamonds. Position the diamonds table facets down to stabilize them across the channel. Bees wax can be applied on the metal if necessary to temporarily keep the diamonds in place. Position the diamonds precisely as they are expected to be spaced after they are set.

STEP 7. Mark the locations of the diamonds. Use a scriber or graver to scratch the metal between the diamonds and at the ends to denote borders (See Fig. 7.2). Make any notations believed necessary to serve as a reminder where each diamond will be set. The border markings will be used as a guide to cutting the bearings. There is very little tolerance acceptable, especially if the diamonds will be set girdle to girdle.

106 INLAID CHANNELS (ROUND DIAMONDS)

Fig. 7.2 Shows round diamonds laid out table facets down over an inlaid channel to mark their locations.

STEP 8. Remove the diamonds. Place the diamonds on a diamond tray in the order that they will be set into the mounting. Mark one end of the mounting and the diamond tray so that later there will be no confusion as to which end of the mounting to start the order. The reasoning behind this is that the size of the bearings might be cut differently for some diamonds. It is imperative to the success of this particular procedure that the diamonds are seated snugly.

STEP 9. Cut the bearings. The bearings are undercut into one wall and vertically cut into the opposite wall. Use a hart bur that is close to the diameter of the diamond but a little smaller. It is better to cut a bearing too small, then make adjustments later rather than to cut it too large. Without applying power, tilt the bur into the side of the channel to be undercut and centered between the border markings. Position the cutting edge at or just below the proposed bearing level (See Fig. 7.3). This is about one and one-half times the distance between the girdle of the diamond to the height of its table facet. At that level the diamond should be seated with its table facet below the surface of the channel after the bearing is cut. On the opposite side of the channel a part of the bur just below the cutting edge should be positioned near the edge of the channel wall.

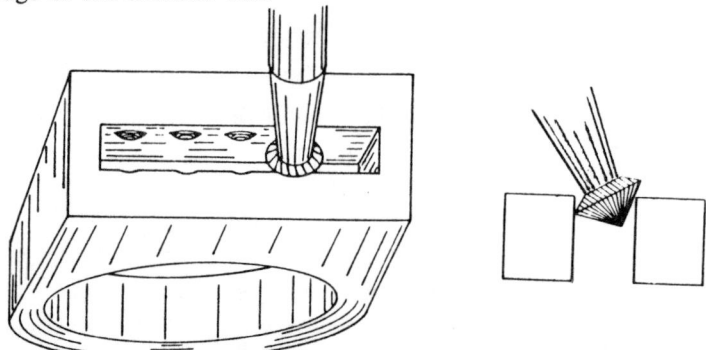

Fig. 7.3 Shows the cutting edge of a hart bur positioned at the proposed bearing level in an inlaid channel to begin undercutting.

INLAID CHANNELS (ROUND DIAMONDS) 107

Hold the mounting in a position where the cutting edge of the hart bur can be seen in the channel. The shaft of the bur should be on a vertical axis to the ends of the channel although it is tilted into a side wall. If the bur shifts from the vertical axis, the bearing will not be cut level. Look into the channel from an end view while holding the mounting and bur steady. The depth of the bur's cutting edge and its position at the edge of the opposite channel wall should be clearly visible. Return to the normal view to check the position of the bur shaft again just before cutting the bearing.

Gradually accelerate power to the bur to make a test cut. While the beginning of the cut is being made, it will be a little tedious to hold the bur in position until it starts to cut into the metal. When a small amount of metal has been shaped and it is felt that the bur can continue with ease, take the bur out of the channel to examine the cut. The beginning of the bearing should be centered between the border lines at the right depth and level.

If no adjustments are necessary continue to cut the bearing but occasionally stop to check the work. Since the walls of an inlaid channel are proportionately farther apart than most channels, the bearings are not cut as far into the walls; therefore, cutting the bearings will require less power. Eventually the bearing should be cut to an equal distance into both channel walls although each bearing is cut differently. Undercut into the channel wall a short distance, then begin pivoting the bur from the undercut to make a vertical cut down the opposite channel wall. The estimated time to begin the vertical movement is when the metal there can be cut without excessive stress on the bur. To do this increase the undercutting slightly while pulling the bur shaft back to near perpendicular position to the channel (See Fig. 7.4). If later the bearing is found to be too high on the channel wall that is not undercut re-insert the bur and cut to a more upright position. It is better to test fit the diamond first because the undercut bearing might be higher than it looks.

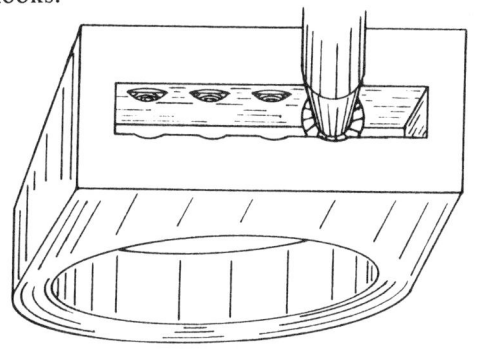

Fig. 7.4 Shows the position of a hart bur in an inlaid channel after undercutting one wall and vertically cutting the opposite wall.

108 INLAID CHANNELS (ROUND DIAMONDS)

After one bearing is cut, trial fit the diamond. If the diamond is centered between the border lines at the right depth and level, then continue to cut other bearings. Make all the undercuts into the same channel wall (See Fig. 7.5). Test the seating arrangements for each bearing that is cut to be sure the diamonds do not overlap. Do not leave any diamonds in the channel while other bearings are being cut. To enlarge a bearing, use a larger hart bur to chase the bearing. If the exact size bur that is needed is not available, then use the previous smaller bur. The smaller bur can enlarge a bearing by maneuvering it to push farther into the undercut.

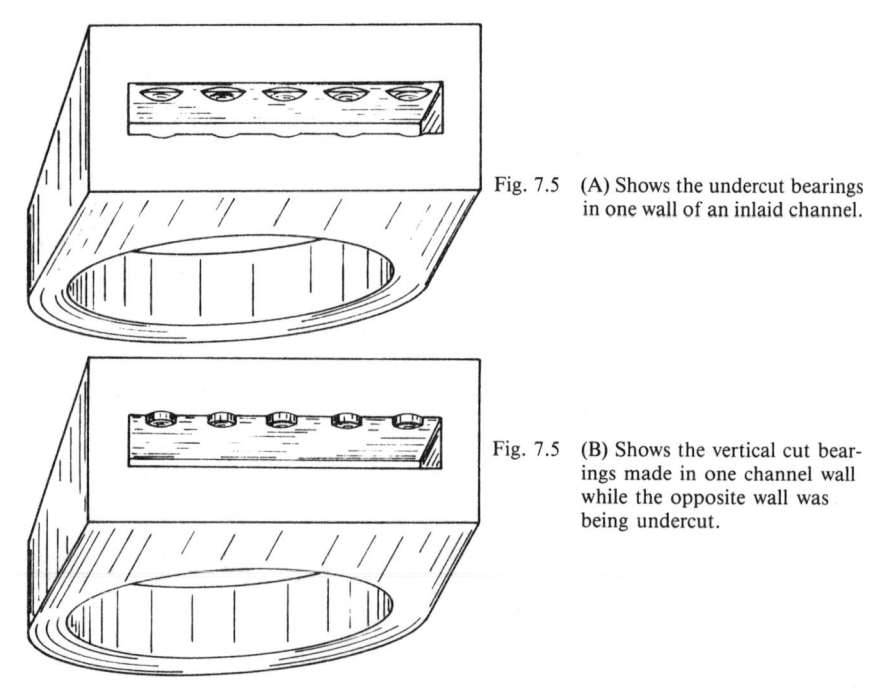

Fig. 7.5 (A) Shows the undercut bearings in one wall of an inlaid channel.

Fig. 7.5 (B) Shows the vertical cut bearings made in one channel wall while the opposite wall was being undercut.

STEP 10. Clean the channel and diamonds. Brush the channel to remove metal particles and other debris. The newly cut bearings will shine if they are clean. Diamonds can be cleaned by tumbling them one at a time between thumb and forefinger or across a cloth stretched over the bench pin.

STEP 11. Seat the diamonds. Replace the diamonds permanently into the channel in the correct order (See Fig. 7.6). They should be critically checked for equal spacing, if not girdle to girdle, and planed across the table facets. This is the last chance to make adjustments to the bearings without affecting the design, so be sure that the arrangement is satisfactory.

INLAID CHANNELS (ROUND DIAMONDS) 109

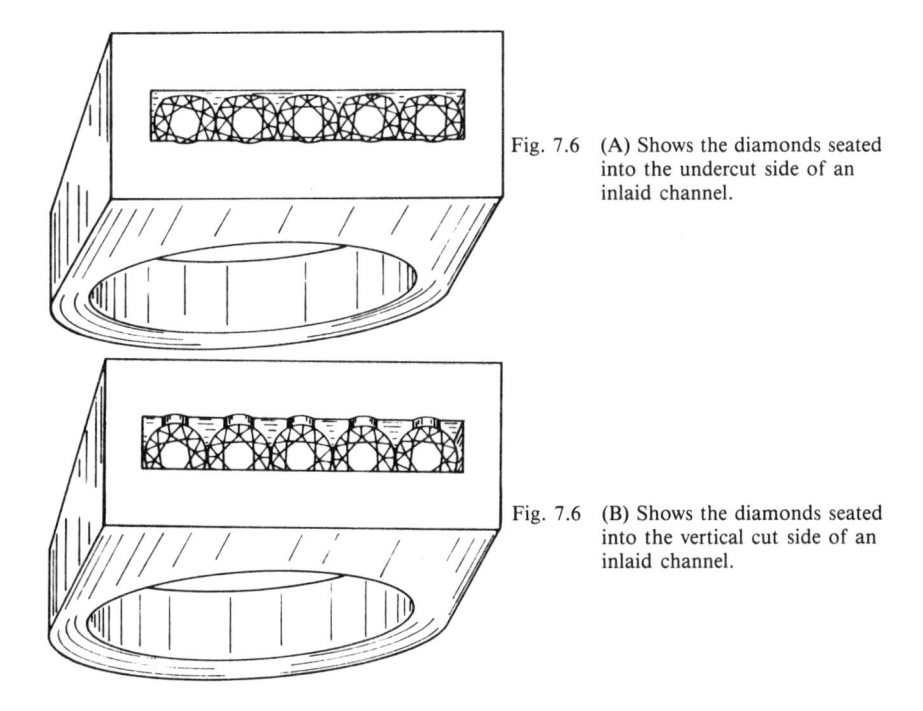

Fig. 7.6 (A) Shows the diamonds seated into the undercut side of an inlaid channel.

Fig. 7.6 (B) Shows the diamonds seated into the vertical cut side of an inlaid channel.

STEP 12. Secure the diamonds. Both sides of the channel will be tapped by a tapping tool and chasing hammer to secure the diamonds. In this case the tip of the tapping tool should be about one and one-half millimeters in diameter. This is a little larger diameter than that used for most channel settings but necessary to minimize indenting the metal. The side of the channel that is not undercut is tapped first, so place the ring on a mandrel or in another fixture in a position where the metal can be seen moving onto the diamonds when it is tapped. If a mandrel is used, make sure the diamonds do not extend to it, and place the ring where the undercut side is at the wider end of the mandrel. This will give a clear view to watch the metal move as it is tapped and help to keep the ring secure on the mandrel.

Begin by holding the tapping tool perpendicular to the metal and just within the edges of the channel as much as possible (See Fig. 7.7). That will help to keep the surface of the mounting flat and minimize beveling the metal along the diamonds. In this case the metal will usually opt to move towards the channel opening rather than into the massive sides of the mounting. Much of the movement depends upon the hardness of the metal. If the metal will not move, then try a narrower tapping tool tip.

110 INLAID CHANNELS (ROUND DIAMONDS)

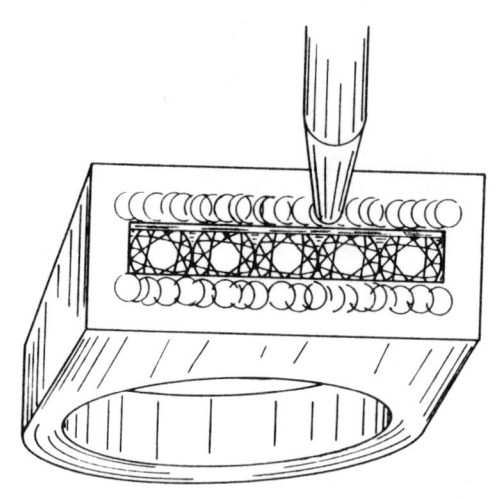

Fig. 7.7 Tapping the metal within the edge of an inlaid channel to secure the diamonds.

Tap the metal along the channel wall that is not undercut first. This should force the metal tight to the girdles of the diamonds on both sides of the channel. Never tap the metal hard. Use a steady pace with the tip of the tapping tool flat to the metal and continually moving adjacent to the channel. Depending upon the hardness of the metal, it could require hundreds of taps. However, once a rhythm is established it should not take long before the diamonds are tight if they were seated snugly to begin with. Furthermore, if the diamonds are seated snugly, the metal does not have to extend far over the crowns of the diamonds to secure them.

Reverse the ring on the mandrel or other fixture to tap the undercut side of the channel. The undercut side should not have to be tapped as much unless the diamonds are loose. If it must be done, then use considerably less force because the stiffness of the metal there is weakened by the undercuts. Other than tapping with less force, the technique is the same as on the side that was undercut. If further assurance that the diamonds will remain tight is needed, then lightly tap the metal with the tip of the tapping tool extending slightly over the edges of the channel walls. This is not recommended unless other measures including burnishing have failed, because it will bevel the metal to the diamonds. The metal adjacent to the diamonds should eventually be trimmed as steep as possible.

STEP 13. Inspect the work up to this stage. Evaluate the position and tightness of the diamonds and the condition of the mounting. Look at the mounting and diamonds from all directions to see if any adjustments are necessary before finishing the metal. From a direct top view, check to see that the metal on each side of the channel covers a portion of the girdles.

INLAID CHANNELS (ROUND DIAMONDS) 111

A diamond can be checked for tightness with bees wax or a narrow probing tool such as a graver or scriber. Bees wax, the safest method, will usually tell if a diamond is tight or loose just by pressing it to the diamond and trying to move it. Be gentle when using the probing tool. Slide the tool down the crown facets of the diamond to an off of the girdle facet. This will push the diamond down if it is loose. If no movement of the diamond is seen, slightly brush the tool up from under the girdle. If there is no movement again, the diamond is probably tight. Be careful when checking the diamonds for tightness with this method because it does not take much to chip a diamond.

STEP 14. Remove indentations from the metal. There will be some distortion caused by the hammering technique. First use a medium cut flat hand file as in STEP 2 to cross file the metal on top of the channel. Be sure that the table facets of the diamonds do not extend above the surface. File as much as necessary to remove indentations without lowering the metal to the table facets. Afterwards file the sides of the mounting to the original design.

STEP 15. Emery the metal to remove file marks. Use NO. 2 emery paper wrapped on an emery stick. An emery stick is used because it will help to keep the metal flat. Emery only what is necessary to remove the file marks. Excessive emerying will cause the edges of the mounting to become rounded.

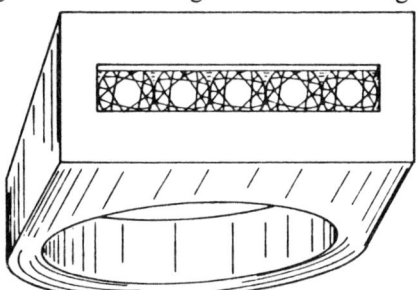

Fig. 7.8 Shows five round diamonds set into an inlaid channel.

STEP 16. Trim the metal in the channel. Use a NO. 40 flat graver with a polished tip. Try not to bevel the metal any more than necessary, but be sure that the edges become straight and smooth. The metal should be steep from the crown facets of the diamonds without sacrificing security. Also, and equally important, the metal on both sides of the channel over the diamonds should be symmetric. This usually requires that more metal from the undercut side of the channel must be removed in order to match the opposite side.

STEP 17. Smooth the metal. Use a NO. 4/0 polishing paper wrapped on an emery stick. Remove all remaining abrasions on the mounting including the emeried areas. The metal should be planed and smooth as much as possible prior to polishing. It is to the diamond setter's advantage that the mounting only need a light buffing to polish it.

7

Inlaid Channels (Square Cut Diamonds)

Setting square cut diamonds into an inlaid channel is one of the most advanced diamond setting procedures. To successfully complete the task requires the highest degrees of persistence, creativity, and mechanical inclination. Prerequisite skills include proficiency in the basic channel setting techniques. Many of the techniques used to set diamonds into the fanciest channel settings are interchangeable. The procedure as discussed and illustrated here is not unique to this design. It is applicable to other contours and straight faceted diamonds including baguettes, emerald cuts and the like. Each phase is intricately arranged to form an array of precious metal and diamonds. Combining the materials into an impressive form is more probable when each phase is performed impressively.

STEP 1. Inspect the mounting. Take a few moments to determine the quality of the mounting. Try to foresee particular problems that might arise because of its design, structure, and chemical make-up. The design alone will give the first impressions of the general procedure that is applicable. Constructural weaknesses and other inadequacies might require the use of special precautionary measures. Some of these are the use of diamond setters cement to pack the mounting and a variety of fixtures such as a mandrel, BenchMate™, padded vice, or engraving block. Lastly, things like the color of gold and the gold content usually give some hint to the vigor necessary to perform the procedure. For instance, yellow gold is commonly softer than white gold, and a higher karat rating usually signifies a more malleable and pliable mounting.

STEP 2. Inspect the diamonds. Like all diamond setting procedures, the diamonds should be of a consistent quality. In this particular procedure the consistency of the diamonds is of the utmost importance. Setting square, baguette, or emerald cuts requires continuous bearings. When channel setting round diamonds, the bearings are commonly cut individually. Slight differences in round cut diamonds can be compensated in many types of channels. On the other hand, channel setting unequal sizes of straight faceted diamonds can be discouraging unless the design is intentionally tapered.

Inspecting the diamonds in this procedure is a two part process. First all diamonds are closely viewed with an eye loupe to reveal certain characteristics. The clarity, cut, color, and carat, all have an effect on the

INLAID CHANNELS (SQUARE CUT DIAMONDS) 113

techniques used to mount them. For example, unfavorable characteristics such as flaws are positioned where they are least exposed. Also the fineness of the facets, and the size of the diamonds will alter a number of procedural techniques. Even the shades of color are dispersed to more or less conspicuous areas of the channel.

A second part of inspecting square cut diamonds is to compare their size and shape. The diamonds are all presumed to be square cut, but the quality of the cuts and the sizes of each could vary. Those variations will affect the techniques used to set them. Despite the diamond setter's efforts, extreme differences in these two qualities will influence the finished design. The best that can be done, besides expert craftsmanship, is to arrange the diamonds in as close to a uniform order as possible. This is begun by placing the diamonds table facets down and in line on a diamond tray. Then, from a top view arrange the diamonds as they will be set into the most attractive order.

STEP 3. Plane the top surface of the mounting. The wide surface of an inlaid mounting frequently has elevations and depressions. These should be leveled early in the procedure. Use a medium cut-flat hand file to apply a cross filing technique until the file marks will cover the surface by one pass. Afterwards, use NO. 2 emery paper wrapped on a flat emery stick to remove the file marks. File marks are removed so that layout markings will be more pronounced without cutting deep into the metal.

STEP 4. Make a notation mark on one side of the diamond tray and the mounting. This is done to avoid reversing the order of diamonds when they are transferred to and from the mounting. The diamonds will be picked up and replaced several times during the procedure. It is important that the layout pattern is not disrupted.

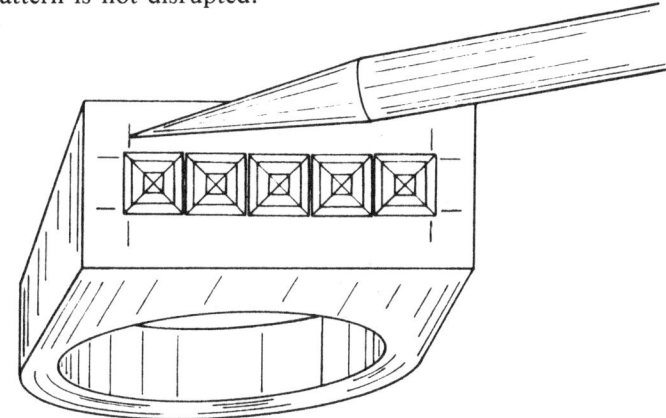

Fig. 8.1 Shows square cut diamonds laid out table facets down to engrave borders for cutting the channel. The marks are engraved about one-half millimeter within the width and length of the diamond formation.

114 INLAID CHANNELS (SQUARE CUT DIAMONDS)

STEP 5. Check the channel dimensions to see if it has to be extended. To do this place the diamonds table facets down on the channel in the pre-arranged order. Position them girdle to girdle in a straight line. Mark the excavation limits of the channel. The channel should be cut to dimensions that are about one-half millimeter less at each wall and the ends than the rectangular pattern formed by the diamonds (See Fig. 8.1). This will leave just enough metal to cut the bearings with gravers later. Bearings are also cut at the ends of the channel. For now concentrate on marking the metal to that size. Use a scriber or pointed graver to engrave the tick marks. Then replace the diamonds back in order on the diamond tray. Use a straight edge or dividers to extend the tick marks straight along the edges of the channel (See Fig. 8.2).

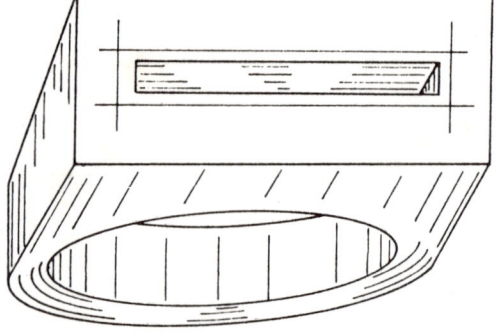

Fig. 8.2 Shows the border marks extended after the diamonds are removed. The channel will be cut to those dimensions.

STEP 6. Trim the channel to the layout markings (See Fig. 8.3). The mounting illustrated in this procedure is open. There is no basin with which to contend. If much metal has to be removed, use a series of cylinder burs to enlarge the channel to the layout markings. It is advisable not to remove any metal from one end of the channel until later in order to avoid removing too much. Later, after all but one or two diamonds are seated, adjust that end of the channel.

After using burs the corners and ends of the channel will still be rounded. These can be further defined by an anglette or knife graver, and a flat graver. The final graver cuts should be made steep down into the channel.

FIg. 8.3 Shows an inlaid channel that has been cut to the border marks.

INLAID CHANNELS (SQUARE CUT DIAMONDS) 115

STEP 7. Cut the bearings. Cutting the bearings for straight faceted diamonds is an intricate venture. Certain burs could be used but only to an extent and usually not recommended. When burs are manipulated to make precision straight cuts, there is always a chance, even in the most skilled hands, that they will get out of control. The bearings can usually be cut straight more precisely by a knife type of graver and a flat graver. A commonly suggested combination is a NO. 1 anglette graver and a NO. 40 flat graver.

In the previous step the channel is trimmed to within one-half millimeter at both sides and the ends of the diamond configuration. The reason for this, being most obvious now, is to minimize the effort needed to cut the bearings by hand. Also, this is a sufficient amount of metal to form bearings and to secure the diamonds.

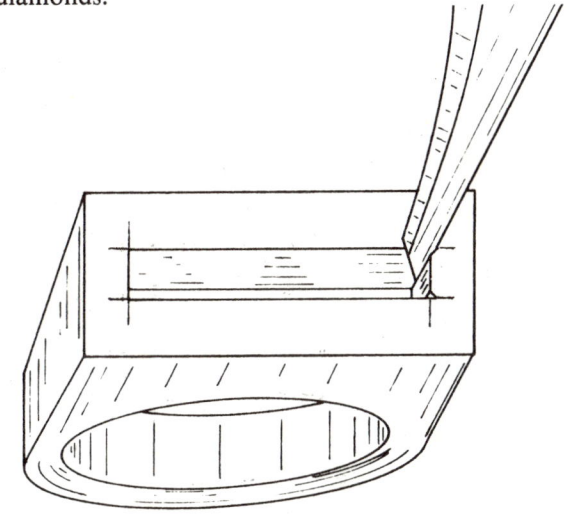

Fig. 8.4 To cut the bearings into an inlaid channel for square cut diamonds begin by cutting the corners at one end with a knife or anglette graver.

There is a reliable process to cut the bearings, but it does not have a specific step by step sequence. The metal is removed gradually by alternating the use of each graver while continually testing the diamonds for fit. In general it is known that one half millimeter of the metal bordering the channel, as it is, will have to be shaped into bearing form. One side will be undercut while the opposite side and the ends will be cut straight down to an equal depth. Then all sides are slanted to a pavilion angle. The depth of the bearing is the level of its vertex that contains the girdles of the diamonds. It should be about one and one-half times the distance from the girdles of the diamonds to the height of their table facets. This will ensure that the diamonds will be seated with the table facets just below the surface of the channel.

116 INLAID CHANNELS (SQUARE CUT DIAMONDS)

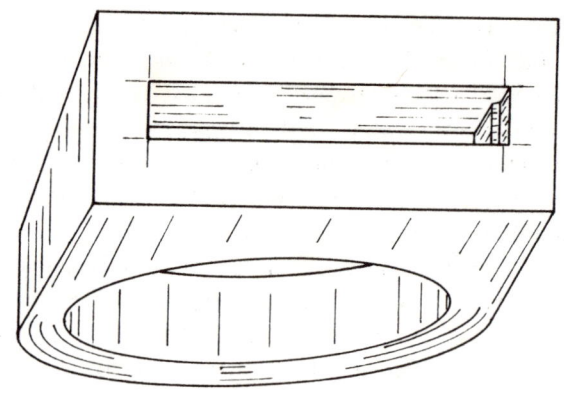

Fig. 8.5 Shows a vertical cut bearing for a square cut diamond at one end of an inlaid channel.

To cut the bearing begin by cutting the corners at the trimmed end of the channel. Use a NO. 1 anglette graver to make the corners steep into the channel (See Fig. 8.4). The cuts should not begin from more than one-half millimeter from the end of the channel nor farther to the side than the diamonds extend. According to the layout, the corners would be bisected beginning at a point that is one-half millimeter from the end and one-half millimeter from each side. On the contrary, this is not always true in actual conditions because layout markings are made without consideration to the undercut. A more accurate assessment is made by placing the diamond to be set there table facet down to see how far to the sides the cuts should begin. The best approach is to cut the corners little by little along with the bearing to avoid over cutting (See Fig. 8.5).

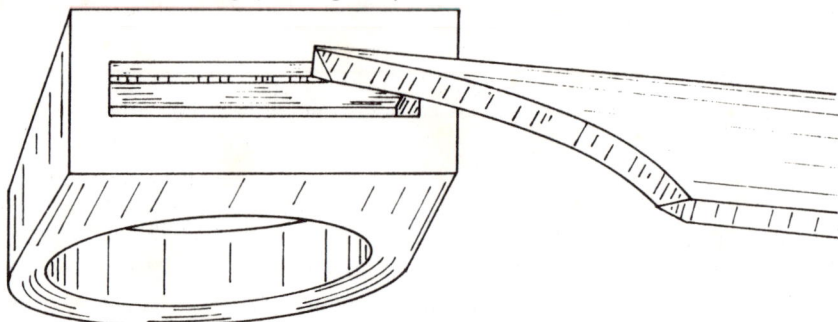

Fig. 8.6 Shows the use of a flat graver to cut a vertical bearing on one side of an inlaid channel.

Cut the bearings lengthwise from a considerable distance along the channel walls to the corners. Use a flat graver to do this (See Fig. 8.6). Begin at the bearing depth and continue to cut from that level. One side will be undercut and the other side, including the end, is cut straight from the bearing level (See Fig. 8.7). Then a pavilion angle is cut on both sides and the end. Do

INLAID CHANNELS (SQUARE CUT DIAMONDS) 117

not neglect the pavilion angle at the end of the channel. The metal there will also be tapped later. A high angle will cause the diamond to set away from the end thereby making it troublesome to hammer the metal to the diamond. Concluding cuts to shape the metal can be made by holding the graver in an upright position to cut down into the channel. To reiterate, all cutting is done gradually by shaving the metal little by little while repeatedly testing the corner diamond for fit.

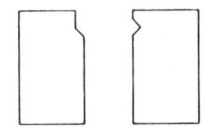

FIg. 8.7   Illustrates details of vertical cut and undercut bearings on opposite walls of an inlaid channel.

After a rough shape of the bearing is formed, more and more attention is given to the corner diamond. Continual use of an eye loupe is necessary to see exactly what metal is keeping the diamond from seating into the undercut wall and down the vertical cut wall. The girdle of the diamond must fit flush to the end of the channel also. To avoid excessive cutting above the bearing level, it will help to trial seat the diamond upside down. If the lower slant of the bearing is reasonably formed, at least it will be known that a seating problem is probably caused by the metal above. Once the diamond will fit upside down, then more attention can be given to the lower bearing and seating the diamond in an upright position.

Some of the most typical seating problems can be corrected by an anglette graver. Keep the corners and the vertex clearly defined (See Fig. 8.8). When the flat graver is used to cut into the corners, metal burrs usually develop there. Before trial fitting the diamond and after the metal has been shaved from the sides, chase the corners with the anglette graver. The vertex of the bearing can become rounded unknowingly. One of the most common mistakes made in this type of channel setting is to cut the channel too wide because a diamond will not set low enough. The solution can usually be attained by either cutting the lower slant of the bearing steeper, deeper, or simply sharpening the vertex by an anglette graver.

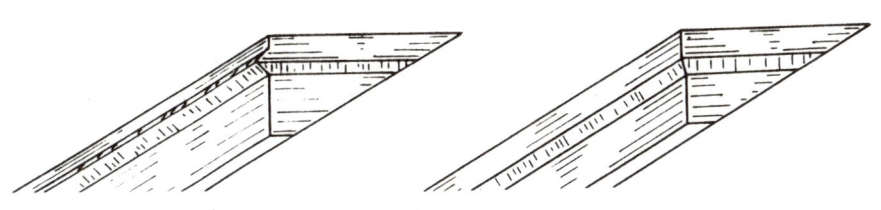

Fig. 8.8   (A) Shows the bearing on one wall of an inlaid channel undercut and the end vertical cut.

Fig. 8.8   (B) Shows the bearing on the opposite channel wall and the end vertically cut.

118 INLAID CHANNELS (SQUARE CUT DIAMONDS)

After all but one or two diamonds are seated, determine if the channel is long enough to contain the remaining diamonds. By this stage the amount of metal that needs to be trimmed should be apparent. If the length of the channel is too short, use the same techniques in STEP 6 to extend it. Afterwards, repeat the process to cut the bearings at that end. When completing the bearing into the opposite corner, remove a few or more of the diamonds to avoid damaging them. The last diamond should barely slip into position.

STEP 8. Inspect and adjust the seating arrangement of the diamonds. They should be setting girdle to girdle below the surface and level. When viewing the line of diamonds from a low angle, the table facets should appear to be on an equal plane. From this view any diamonds that are not setting level will immediately be recognized by the position of its table facet compared to the others. That is unless all of the diamonds are slanted in the bearing. Any noticeable problems should be confronted now before the diamonds are secured.

STEP 9. Secure the diamonds. The diamonds are secured by tapping the surrounding metal onto them by a tapping tool and chasing hammer. Use a tapping tool that tapers to a flat circular tip that is about one and one-half millimeters in diameter. A smaller diameter could cause serious indentations. The metal will not move readily if it is tapped by a larger diameter tip.

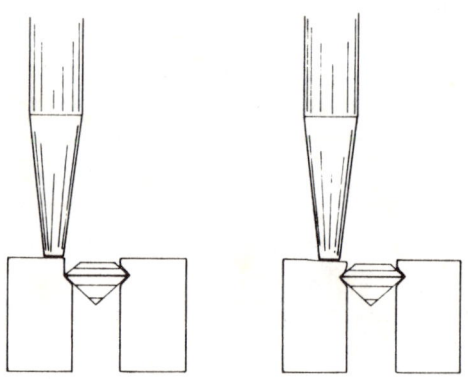

Fig. 8.9 Shows the position to hold a tapping tool and the action to secure a square cut diamond into an inlaid channel.

Place the ring on a sturdy fixture that will hold the ring tight when it is tapped. First tap the metal on the side of the channel that is not undercut. Hold the tapping tool perpendicular to the metal and flush to the edge (See Fig. 8.9). Keep the tool moving between each tap along the metal beyond the end diamonds just past the corners. Tap with a swift rhythmic speed rather than pounding. Eventually the metal should move to secure the diamonds at the girdle facets. Occasionally stop and check the progress with an eye

INLAID CHANNELS (SQUARE CUT DIAMONDS) 119

loupe to see if the metal is actually covering the girdles of the diamonds. Do not attempt to tap the metal flush to the crown facets at this time. That metal will be attended to later by the less risky technique of burnishing. If the metal will absolutely not move, then position the tip partially over the inner edge of the channel walls. The metal will move easier but also have the unfavorable effect of beveling. When the diamonds are tight, repeat the tapping technique to the undercut side of the channel and the ends (See Fig. 8.10). Upon completion all the metal should be closed over the girdles of the diamonds.

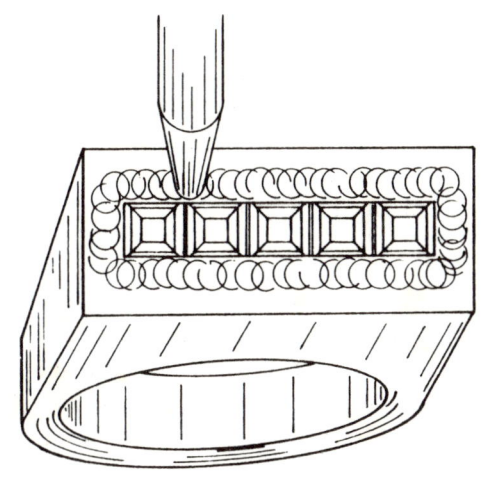

Fig. 8.10 Shows square cut diamonds being secured into an inlaid channel by tapping the metal beyond the sides and the ends of the channel.

STEP 10. Fill in depressions developed by tapping. When the diamonds are secured by tapping, the metal will be beveled more or less from the diamonds to the surface of the mounting and indented. To fill in some of this depression, tap the metal around the channel adjacent to the previously tapped metal. Use a tapping tool that has a larger diameter tip (about one and one-half to two millimeters). Gold, being malleable as it is, can be redistributed closer to the edge of the channel by doing this. The technique is also helpful to move troublesome metal at the corners of the channel over the diamonds. When the best that can be done has been done, go over the indented areas with the larger tip-tapping tool to smooth indentations as much as possible. Keep in mind that later the surface of the metal will be filed to the depth of the deepest indentation.

STEP 11. Burnish the edges of the channel onto the diamonds. Unless the metal is hammered too much, a gap is expected between the crown facets of the diamonds and the edges of the channel metal. Burnish the metal with a tool similar to a prong pusher that has a flat rectangular tip about one millimeter by two millimeters. The length of the tip is important for control

120 INLAID CHANNELS (SQUARE CUT DIAMONDS)

to keep the tool from slipping onto the diamonds. Its width is narrow for viewing purposes.

Hold the tool low to the metal and at a horizontal angle that will allow a lengthwise movement. The tip is positioned upright and pushed along the metal close to but not touching the diamonds (See Fig. 8.11). If the tip contacts the diamonds, they could become chipped or the metal could be burnished too much. Part of the skill involved is knowing when to stop. Push the tip repeatedly, without too much force, in one direction as much as necessary. The direction will have to be reversed for short distances at opposite corners.

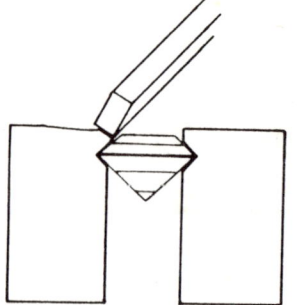

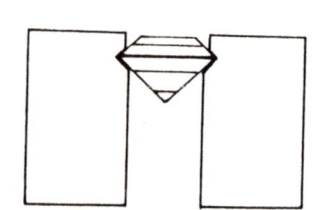

Fig. 8.11 Illustrates the use of a flat-rectangular tipped tool to burnish inlaid channel metal onto square cut diamonds.

STEP 12. Remove indentations. Deep indentations should be filled in by tapping the metal adjacent to and towards them as was done in STEP 10. Then use a medium cut-flat hand file. File the metal directly over the channel if the diamonds are below the surface. The entire top surface of the mounting should be filed at cross angles until all dents are removed and the complete surface can be evenly filed by one pass. While doing this, occasionally brush the channel clear of filings and check to see that the diamonds are below the surface.

STEP 13. Trim the channel. Use a NO. 40 flat graver that has a polished tip to straighten the burnished metal. Hold the graver at a low angle with the tip upright. It is best for cosmetic purposes to shave the metal perpendicular to the channel. Beveling the metal from the diamonds is acceptable, but it does not result in a finish that is as attractive. The corners are tricky because the graver tip must be held at the same angle while reversing the cutting direction. To avoid serious cutting mistakes, shave the metal a little at a time and continually stop to brush the metal and inspect the progress.

STEP 14. Remove file marks. Use NO. 2 emery paper wrapped on an emery stick to remove the file marks. Be careful not to emery too much

INLAID CHANNELS (SQUARE CUT DIAMONDS) 121

because the edges of the metal will become rounded. It often helps to place the emery paper on a flat surface and draw the mounting across it a few times by hand.

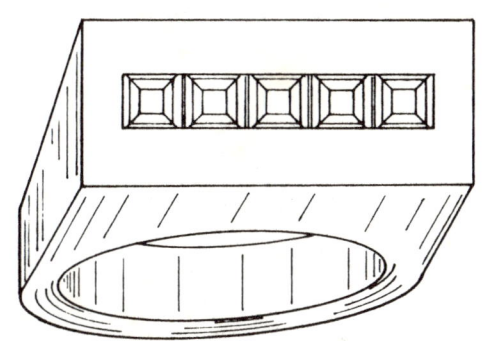

Fig. 8.12 Shows five square cut diamonds set into an inlaid channel.

STEP 15. Smooth the metal. Use NO.4/0 polishing paper wrapped on an emery stick or placed on a flat surface as in the previous step to smooth the metal further. Do not use rubber wheels on the surface of this particular mounting because the wheels will rub depressions in the metal.

CHANNEL SETTING PROBLEMS AND SOLUTIONS

PROBLEM 1 (Fig. 1): A prong cluster obstructing normal channel setting techniques.

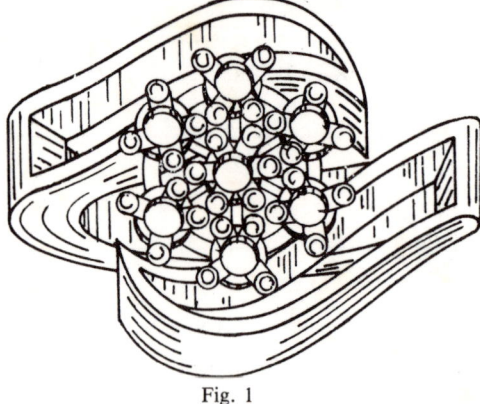

Fig. 1

SOLUTION 1: The prong setting has probably been soldered in place. See if it can be removed so the diamonds can be set into the channels first. A center setting in this type of mounting is usually tack soldered in only two or four spots. A jewelry mechanic (if available) should be able to remove the setting in just a few minutes. It will allow the channels to be set with greater perfection and save much time overall. After the diamonds are channel set polish the area between the channels before re-assembling the prong setting.

SOLUTION 2: If the center setting cannot be dis-assembled from the mounting, then bend the prongs that extend over the channel inward. The prongs should be pliable enough to bend over and back a couple times without breaking. Then channel set the diamonds using the procedure applicable to curvature designs beginning on page 79. When securing the diamonds the use of pliers will be limited. The channel metal that adjoins the center setting might have to be tapped onto the diamonds by a tapping tool. Because of positioning problems the tip of the tapping tool might have to be very narrow.

PROBLEM 2 (Fig. 2): Structural rings attached between the channel walls. These rings, or a similarly constructed undergallery, are designed to provide strength to the channel, and can be used as "rests" for the pavilion facets of the diamonds. Occasionally they are positioned too high in the channel. In that case they have to be machined without destroying them so the diamonds can be set low.

CHANNEL SETTING PROBLEMS AND SOLUTIONS 123

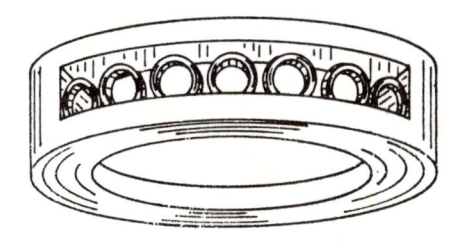

Fig. 2

SOLUTION: Use a bud bur or setting bur to cut a taper into the rings. That will enlarge the holes so the diamonds can fit lower. Also, a taper cut will minimize the amount of metal that has to be removed from them. Keep the holes spaced appropriately for the diamonds and be careful not to remove any more metal than necessary.

PROBLEM 3 (Fig. 3): The channel metal is too massive to bend by pliers and usual hammering/tapping attempts have failed because the metal is also too stiff.

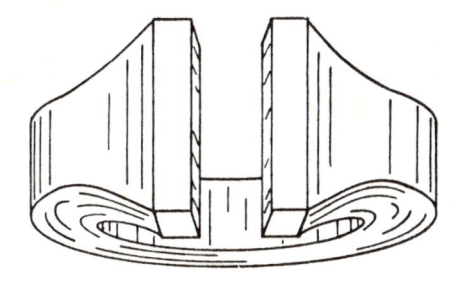

Fig. 3

SOLUTION: Whether in a case such as the illustrated mounting, or a similar situation, the simplest solution it to anneal the mounting. That is, unless it has been soldered near the channel. An alternative is to position the tip of the tapping tool midway over the edge of the channel. If the metal still will not move use a tapping tool that has a very small diameter tip (about three-fourths millimeter). Such a small tip is risky to use near diamonds, severely indents the metal, and prohibits a steep bevel of metal from the diamonds; however, as a last resort it is usually effective to secure diamonds into a channel when all else fails.

SERIAL PROCEDURES

The techniques to channel set diamonds into adjoining rows are basically a mere repetition to setting a single row of the same type. The difference is that completing one row is only a part of a larger procedure. Techniques

124 CHANNEL SETTING PROBLEMS AND SOLUTIONS

can be useless if they are not organized. Three different serial procedures are described in the following problems.

PROBLEM 4: Setting a series of rows that are positioned on an arched plane and have narrow walls (Fig. 4).

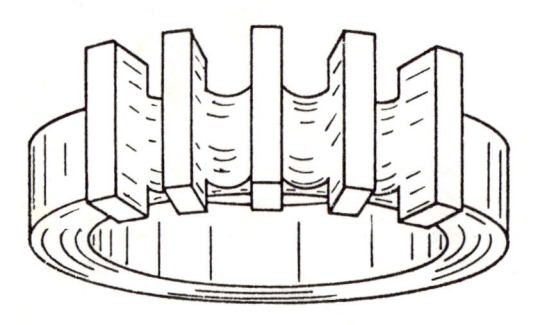

Fig. 4

SOLUTION: Begin at one end of the mounting. Undercut the bearings into the wall at the extreme end and vertical cut the bearings into the opposite wall. Do not cut more than one-third into the inner walls because the metal will be shared by the adjacent row. Secure that row of diamonds but do not remove any metal by filing, emering, etc., until all of the rows have been secured. Next, set the adjacent row of diamonds in a similar manner making sure that the bearings are undercut into the other side of the same wall that was vertically cut. In effect, all the undercut bearings will be towards the same direction on the mounting. Continue the same sequence one row at a time until all the diamonds are secure. Afterwards, make any corrections necessary for security and levelness, then file and emery the mounting to finish it.

PROBLEM 5: Channel setting a series of rows that are stepped up on the mounting and have narrow walls (Fig. 5).

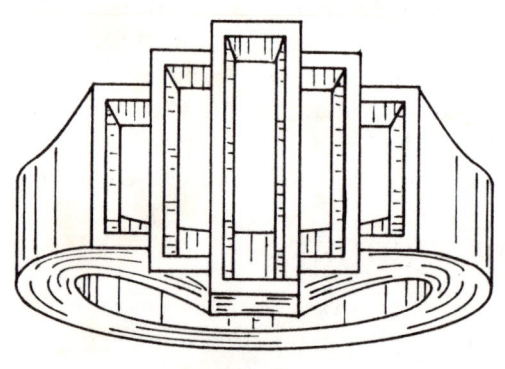

Fig. 5

CHANNEL SETTING PROBLEMS AND SOLUTIONS 125

SOLUTION: Set the top channel first then work down toward both ends of the mounting. The bearings for the top channel may be undercut, vertically cut, or a combination of both. Bearings for other rows must be undercut into the walls closest to the center and vertically cut into the opposite walls.

PROBLEM 6: A series of channel rows are on a straight plane across the mounting and have wide walls (Fig. 6).

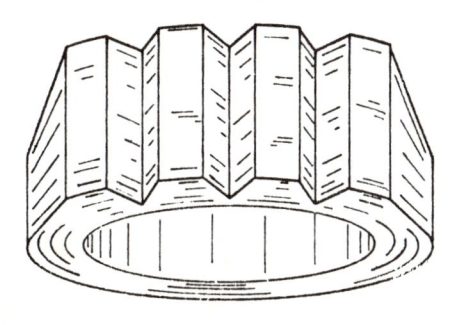

Fig. 6

SOLUTION: Set the diamonds into the center channel first by following the procedures of inlaid channels beginning on page 104. Do not finish the metal until the diamonds are secured into all the rows. Then channel set the side rows by undercutting bearings into the center metal. This is usually necessary because tapping could affect the previously secured center row. Afterwards, trim and finish the mounting.

PROBLEM 7 (Fig. 7A): Bearings can be cut into a channel to contain the girdle and pavilion facets of the diamonds but the channel above the bearing level is too wide and the walls are too massive to be adjusted.

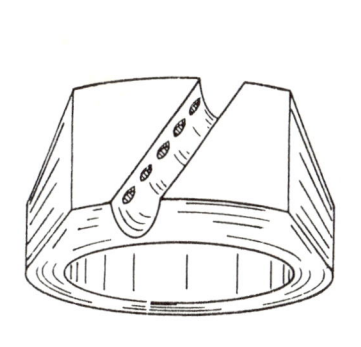

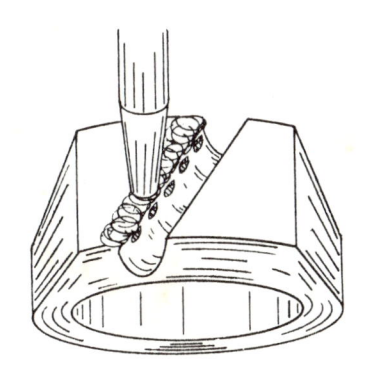

Fig. 7A   Fig. 7B

126 CHANNEL SETTING PROBLEMS AND SOLUTIONS

SOLUTION: With the diamonds removed, tap the metal on one side over the channel (Fig. 7B). That will provide a ledge to keep the diamonds from lifting out. Tap the metal far enough that consistent undercut bearings can be made in order to keep the diamonds level. Then seat the diamonds and tap the opposite side to secure them.

PROBLEM 8: The channel length is too short.

SOLUTION 1—For rectangular channels: Lay out the diamonds to mark the appropriate channel dimensions with a scriber. Then use dividers to clarify the borders. Roughly extend the length with a cylinder bur. Then use a knife or anglette graver to trim the corners. Afterwards, square the metal into the corners with a flat graver.

SOLUTION 2—For tapered channels: Use a tapered cylinder bur to rough cut the metal to the ends. Machining by the tapered cylinder bur may be satisfactory unless the ends are to be pointed. If so, then trim the metal with a knife graver and a flat graver.

PROBLEM 9: Traditional methods to secure the diamonds into curvature channels are not practical in some cases. This commonly occurs when channel setting diamonds into loupes of curves. To secure diamonds into a curved channel the metal usually has to be bent from the inner arc wall towards the outer arc. Neither pliers nor a tapping tool can always be used effectively because of positioning. Even though the channel wall at the outer arc is accessible, attempts to secure the diamonds tight from that metal often has negative results.

SOLUTION: Use the same principles to secure channel set diamonds into curvature designs (See CURVED CHANNELS page 79), but innovate a technique that is applicable to the circumstances. For example, a narrow shaped round graver can often be inserted into a tangled series of curved channels for leverage to burnish the metal onto the diamonds.

PROBLEM 10: The channel metal springs back when trying to bend it onto the diamonds.

SOLUTION: This case is typical when trying to bend the outer wall of a curved channel. Most curved channels can be secured only by metal from the wall at the inner arc of the channel. If a curvature contour is not the case then try filing the top of the channel walls to thin the metal, then tap the metal onto the diamonds. Some compromise to the design might have to be sacrificed. Do not file the metal so thin that security is jeopardized.

PROBLEM 11: Remove a channel set diamond. This occurrence is most often necessary when a diamond is either poorly set or has become chipped.

CHANNEL SETTING PROBLEMS AND SOLUTIONS 127

SOLUTION 1—Removing a diamond from a channel that has narrow walls: Use a flat graver with a strong shaped tip to wedge the metal from the diamond. Use a large size graver that is not sharp to avoid cutting the metal. The idea is to bend the metal back, not to remove it. Push directly into the channel wall at a low angle just above the diamond. Try to keep pressure away from the diamond rather than on it. Do not use the diamond as a leverage.

SOLUTION 2—Removing a diamond from a channel with walls that cannot be moved: Use a sharp knife and flat graver to shave the metal from the diamond on one side of the channel. Try not to remove any more metal than absolutely necessary to remove the diamond. When the girdle facet is clearly visible from a direct top view use a probing tool to push the diamond out from underneath the channel. Do not push hard. If the diamond will not come out easily then remove more metal and try again.

PROBLEM 12: Straightening a channel set diamond.

SOLUTION: Many channel set diamonds that have been set unlevel can be corrected by loosening the channel wall where the diamond is seated lower. The metal is pried back as described in problem 11 to loosen and adjust the diamond without removing it. Afterwards, bend the opposite wall farther onto the diamond. If the diamond can not be seated into a level position then it will have to be removed to recut the bearing.

PROBLEM 13: Replacing a diamond into a channel.

SOLUTION: The solution to replace a channel set diamond is usually not as basic as the procedure that was originally used to set it. Other diamonds are already secured adjacent to the vacant bearing and the metal has probably been trimmed to a minimum. First straighten the channel walls to as near an original condition as possible. If the bearing must be recut then manipulate smaller bearing cutting burs in a circular motion at low speeds to avoid chipping the adjacent diamonds.

PROBLEM 14: Removing a broken drill tip that is submerged below the surface of the metal.

SOLUTION: First drill completely through the metal adjacent to the broken fragment. Sometimes a pointed graver can then be used to pick the fragment loose. If not, then use a narrow tapered punch made from a bur shaft to force the fragment out. To do this the metal might have to first be burred out under the plate by a small bud bur until it hits the drill fragment. Then punch the fragment from the underside of the plate to force it out. Once the drill is forced above the surface twist it counter clockwise with chain nose pliers to remove it.

PROBLEM 15: Smoothing deep indentations in metal. Filing is not always the answer to remove severe abrasions. There might be a limited amount of metal above the diamonds. Either the design or security of diamonds could be affected.

SOLUTION: Use a tapping tool that has a large diameter tip (about one and one-half to two millimeters) to tap the metal flat. Assuming that the metal is gold, it will move from elevations to fill in depressions. Afterwards, plane the metal with an appropriately shaped-fine cut file followed by NO. 2 emery paper, then NO. 4/0 polishing paper.

Afterword

Inevitably just when a craftsman becomes comfortable with the skills obtained to believe that all techniques are mastered, there will be a frustrating experience. It will happen time and time again. Granted, some objectives are impossible, but carrying that attitude only hinders progress in the craft. When encountered by a seemingly impractical and ultimately defeating task, step back and review the situation. Leave the workbench if necessary to collect thoughts and consider all the alternatives. Keep in mind that there are multiple techniques and tools available, and more yet to be innovated, that can be applied to obtain the same result. One of the best tools is communication. It requires humbleness rather than arrogance. Do not be reluctant to seek advice, even from those of interrelated departments. There is always someone who knows something that you do not and vice versa. The finest craftsmen do not lose spirit for long from what would otherwise be a disturbing experience. Instead, they thrive on unusual events to stimulate their own learning process.

DIAMOND SETTING SCHOOLS

ALBERTA COLLEGE OF ART
1407-14th Ave. N.W.
Calgary Alberta T2N 4R3

BOWMAN TECHNICAL SCHOOL
220 West King Street
Lancaster, PA. 17603
717-397-7484

CHARLES STUART
SCHOOL OF DIAMOND SETTING
1420 Kings Hwy.
Brooklyn, NY. 11229

DRY RIDGE
DIAMOND SETTING SCHOOL
P.O. Box 18814
Erlanger, KY. 41018

1ST INTERNATIONAL INSTITUTE
OF JEWELRY GOLDSMITHS
25255 Southfield Road
Southfield, MI. 48075
313-569-0022

GEM CITY COLLEGE
P.O. Box 179
Quincy, ILL. 62301
217-222-0391

GEMOLOGICAL INSTITUTE
OF AMERICA
P.O. Box 2110
Santa Monica, CA. 90406
213-829-2991
800-421-7250

GEORGE BROWN COLLEGE OF
APPLIED ARTS & TECH.
Box 1015 Station B
Toronto, Canada M5T 2T9

HOLLAND SCHOOL
FOR JEWELERS
231 Broad Box 882
Selma, AL. 36701
205-872-3421

INSTITUTE OF
JEWELRY TRAINING
3901 Norwood Ave. #B
Sacramento, CA. 95838
916-648-1122

JEWELERS INSTITUTE
OF AMERICA
P.O. Box 66
Statesboro, GA. 30458

THE JEWELRY INSTITUTE
40 Sims Ave.
Providence, RI. 02909
401-351-0700

KANSAS CITY SCHOOL
OF WATCHMAKING
(also has diamond setting classes)
4524 Main
Kansas City, MO. 64111
816-931-5522

MOHAVE COMMUNITY COLLEGE
1977 W. Acoma Blvd.
Lake Havasu City, AZ. 86403

NORTH BENNET STREET SCHOOL
39 N. Bennet St. Box J.
Boston, MA. 02113
617-227-0155

PARIS JUNIOR COLLEGE
DIV. OF JEWELRY TECH.
2400 Clarksville
Paris, TX. 75460
214-785-7661

RAY SCHOW'S SCHOOL
OF DIAMOND SETTING
1826 N.E. 122nd
Portland, OR. 97230
503-255-1116

REVERE ACADEMY OF
JEWELRY ARTS
760 Market St. #939
San Francisco, CA. 94102
415-391-4179

DIAMOND SETTING SCHOOLS (cont.)

SOUTH TEXAS SCHOOL
FOR JEWELERS
3111-A Nacagdoches
San Antonio, TX. 78217
512-653-8951

STEWARTS INTERNATIONAL
SCHOOL FOR JEWELERS
651 Indiantown Rd.
Jupiter, FL. 33458
305-746-7586

STUDIO JEWELERS LTD.
32 East 31st Street
New York, NY. 10016
212-686-1944

TRENTON JEWELRY
SCHOOLS
2505 Popular Ave.
Memphis, TN. 38112
TN. 800-582-9181
Others 800-238-9226

SUGGESTED READINGS

Bauer, Max, *Precious Stones,* Vol. 1, Trans. L. J. Spencer (1904; rpt. New York; Dover Publications, Inc. 1968)
   Contains authoritative information on diamonds.

Budinski, Kenneth G., *Engineering Materials: Properties And Selection* (Reston, Virginia: Reston Publishing Co. Inc. 1979).
   This book has very good sections covering the chemistry of metals.

Feirer, John L. and Lindbeck, John R., *Metalwork,* 2nd ed., (Peoria, Illinois: Chas. A. Bennett Co., Inc. 1970).
   Thorough metalworking book that teaches how to design, plan, and carry out a project.

Glaser, Don, *Videotape—Engraving Methods & Techniques.* (Emporia, KS: Glendo Corp. 1986).
   Shows many technical "secrets" used by engravers throughout the world; approximately 4 hours.

Glaser, Don, *Videotape—Instruction And Demonstration: Engraving, Jewelry making, Wood carving, Tool preparation, etc.* (Emporia, KS: Glendo Corp. 1984).
   This videotape is highly recommended for both novice and advanced diamond setters. Includes technical information of graver preparation and use; approximately 1 hour-50 minutes.

Hardy, Allen R. and Bowman, John J., *The Jewelry Engravers Manual* (New York: Van Nostrand-Reinhold Co., 1976).
   An excellent reference source for graver preparation and use.

Hemard, Larry, *Creative Jewelry Making* (Garden City, New York: Doubleday & Co. Inc., 1975).
   Fine photography of actual bead setting. Includes sections with line drawings of channel setting baguettes, star setting, and gypsy setting.

Jarvis, Charles A., *Jewelry Manufacture and Repair* (New York: Bonanza Books, 1979).
   Good sections on preparing plates and settings for diamond setting; includes drilling and laying out diamonds. Also a section on eternity rings.

McCreight, Tim, *Metalworking For Jewelry: Tools, Materials, Techniques* New York: Van Nostrand-Reinhold Co., 1979).
   Among other valuable information applicable to diamond setting this book describes in detail the techniques of moving metal.

SUGGESTED READINGS (cont.)

Wooding, Robert R., *Bead Setting Diamonds With Pave' Applications* (Erlanger, KY: Dry Ridge Co. 1985).
    Bead setting diamonds is the exclusive subject of the text. The instruction is advanced diamond setting with over 250 photographs of actual bead setting diamonds.

Wooding, Robert R., *Diamond Setting: The Professional Approach* (Erlanger, KY: Dry Ridge Co., 1984).
    This book was written to teach diamond setting. It is basic enough to be understood by an apprentice, yet sufficiently in depth to benefit an experienced diamond setter.

INDEX

Afterword, 129
anglette graver (use of), 24, 33
Angular Channels, 96-103
Basic Closed Channel, 53-67
Basic Open Channel, 70-78
basin, 27, 59-61, 68-69
Bearing Cutting Tools And Techniques, 27
Bearing Depth, 26
bearing level, 27
bearing dimensions, 27, 31
bud bur (use of) 20-22, 58-59
Burnishing, 46, 84, 120
center points, 17-18, 57
channel setting defined, 3
Channel Setting Problems And Solutions, 122-128
Channel Setting Techniques, 1-47
Chasing Hammer, 41, 42
closed channel, 27
Compatibility Of Mounting And Diamonds, 8
Counter Ream The Holes, 22
cross filing, 15
crown facets, 8
culet, 8
Curved Channels, 79-86
Cut The Bearing, 26
Cut The Channel, 19, 23
Depth of Channel, 9
Design inspection, 5
diamond (facets of), 8, cleaning, 90
Diamond Setting Schools, 131-132
diamond tray, 81
dividers (use of), 21, 22, 56, 57, 59, 89
Drill The Holes, 19, 57-58
Finishing, 45-47

Fixtures For Hammering/Tapping, 42
flat graver (use of), 24, 30, 32, 33, 69, 77, 86, 94, 116
girdle facet, 8
hammer setting, 40, 96, 100
Hammering/Tapping, 40-42, 101, 109
hart bur (use of), 31
Illustrated Channel Setting Procedures, 50-121
Inlaid Channels (round diamonds), 104-111
Inlaid Channels (square cut diamonds, 112-121
Inspect The Diamonds, 7
Inspect The Mounting, 5
Inspection phase, 4
knife edge pumice wheel (use of), 95
knife graver (use of), 24, 68
Layout phase, 12
Layout Preparations, 13
Layout The Diamonds, 15
Length inspection, 10
mandrel (use of), 42, 100
Mark The Layout, 16
open channel, 27, 70
pavilion facets, 8
Pliers (use of), 37-40
Problem Solving, 34, 122-128
Procedures (see Contents)
"pulling holes", 21, 59
Quality inspection, 6
reaming holes, 22, 59-60
Remove Indentations, 45
saw (use of), 60
Schools, 131-132
scriber (use of), 17-18, 56-57, 72, 90, 113

INDEX (cont.)

Seat The Diamonds, 33
Seating Recommendations, 34
Secure The Diamonds, 37
Serial Procedures, 123
setting bur (use of), 20, 22-23, 29, 60
Smooth The Metal, 47
Square Cut Diamonds (setting of) 68-69, 112-121
Strength inspection, 6
Suggested Readings, 133-134
Supplement (auxillary illustrations), 68-69
table facet, 8

Taper Bore The Holes, 20-58
Tapered Channels, 87-95
Tapping Tool (use of), 35, 40, 42, 65, 76, 85, 93, 101, 102, 110
Testing A Diamond For Security, 43, 75
Trim The Design, 46
Undercutting, 30, for round diamonds, 31, for square cut diamonds, 32
Vertex (of a bearing), 26, 59
Vertical Cut Bearings, 28
wheel bur (use of), 24, 61
Width inspection, 9

Other Books By Robert R. Wooding

Now You Can Set Diamonds On The Premises

If you want it done right...On time...If quality counts... This 176-page book by a diamond setting instructor will show you how. See why thousands have already been sold.

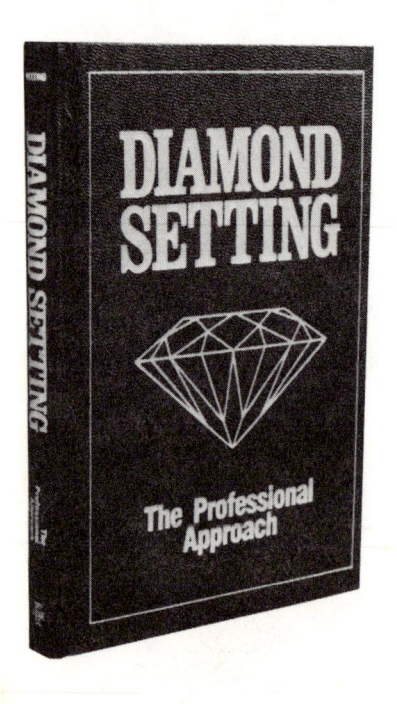

CONTENTS:

- Tools — How to use them
- Pin Point Setting
- Prong Setting
- Setting Fancy Cut Diamonds
- Bezel Setting
- Channel Setting
- Fishtail Setting
- Bead Setting
- and much more...

ONLY
$**29**^{95}$

- Avoid delays and problems from outside labor
- Teaches basic diamond setting to advanced techniques
- Easy to follow-step by step-illustrated procedures
- Reveals tricks of the trade kept secrets by the craftsmen

COMPLETE DIAMOND SETTING BOOK FROM BASIC TO ADVANCED!

CONTENTS

1 Introduction 1
   Evolution of diamond setting to a specialized craft 1
   Personal requirements 3
   The diamond 4
2 Required tool list: Description and purpose 6
3 Selected tool preparation and use 31
   Heat treating steel 31
      Annealing 32
      Hardening 32
      Tempering 33
   Gravers 33
      Assembling graver and handle 33
      Shaping gravers 34
         Graver shaping specifications 36
         Helpful considerations to shape gravers ... 36
      Sharpening gravers 37
      Polishing flat graver tips 39
         Procedure to polish the tip of a flat graver 39
   Filing 42
      Helpful considerations when filing 42
   Sawing 43
   Drilling 43
      Why drills work 44
      Sharpening drills 44
   Burs: How to use them 45
   Re-shaping beading tools 46
      Procedure to re-shape beading tools 46
   Emery stick making 47
      Procedure to make an emery stick 47
   Cement stick making 48
      Applying pendants to the cement stick 49
      Applying earrings to the stick 50
      Applying brooches and pins to the cement stick ... 50
   Bees Wax: How to use it 51
4 Pin-point setting 53
   Setting a diamond into a pin-point setting 53
   Procedure to set a diamond into
      a pin-point setting 54
   Alternate procedures of pin-point setting and
      relevant information 60
      Selecting the correct size bur 60
      Cutting the bearing 60
      Securing the diamond 61
   Undercutting 63
      Undercutting procedure 63
   Setting pin-point clusters 67
5 Prong setting round diamonds 68
   Four-prong setting 68
   Prong-setting procedures 68
      A. Level the prongs 68
      B. Cut the bearing 71
         Alternate procedures to cut the bearing ... 72
         1. Cut the bearing with a hart bur 72
         2. Cut the bearing with a setting bur 74
         3. Cut the bearing with a flat graver 75
         4. Cut the bearing with a needle file 76
      C. Seat the diamond 76
         Using chain-nose pliers to seat a diamond 78
      D. Tighten the diamond 79
         1. Tighten the diamond with a prong pusher .. 79

      2. Tighten the diamond with
         chain-nose pliers 81
      E. Shape the prong tips 82
         1. Bead the prong tips 82
         2. File the prong tips 82
      F. Clean up the work 83
   Prong clusters 83
   Split-prong settings 85
   Miracle settings 86
   Mulitiple-prong settings 86
6 Prong setting fancy-cut diamonds 87
   Oval-cut diamonds 87
   Marquis-cut diamonds 91
   Procedure to set a marquis diamond into a
      common prong setting 91
   Procedure to set a marquis diamond into
      die-struck V-shape prongs 98
   Procedure to set a marquis diamond into
      cast V-shape prongs 103
   Heart and pear-cut diamonds 107
   Emerald-cut diamonds 107
      Procedure to set emerald-cut diamonds 108
   Baguette diamonds 111
      Procedure to set baguette diamonds 111
      Cut the bearing 111
      Secure the diamond 114
7 Bezel setting — Gypsy setting 117
   Bezel setting round diamonds 117
      Procedures to bezel set a round diamond 117
   Bezel setting fancy-cut diamonds 125
      Procedure to bezel set a pear-cut diamond 125
   Gypsy setting 131
8 Channel setting 133
   Channel setting round diamonds 133
      Procedure to channel set diamonds 133
   Channel setting square-cut diamonds 142
9 Fishtail setting — Bar-top setting 144
   Setting a center diamond into a fishtail setting 144
   Procedure to set a center diamond into
      a fishtail setting 145
   Setting melee into fishtail settings 149
      Procedure to set melee into fishtail settings 150
   Bar-top settings 153
   Procedure to set a diamond into a
      bar-top setting 153
10 Bead setting 155
   Bead setting center diamonds 155
      Procedure to bead set a center diamond 156
      Drill and bore a hole 156
      Cut the bearing and seat the diamond 158
      "Raise the beads" 160
      Rough cut the surrounding metal 162
      "Round off the beads" 164
      Bright cut the metal bordering the diamond ... 165
   Bead setting clusters 167
   Procedure to bead set a seven-diamond
      round cluster 167
Suggested readings 173
Diamond Setting Schools 174
Index 175

Other Books By Robert R. Wooding

BEAD SETTING DIAMONDS ISN'T DIFFICULT

(The secret is in the procedure and the use of tools)

This book gives answers to problems that others have spent years to solve!

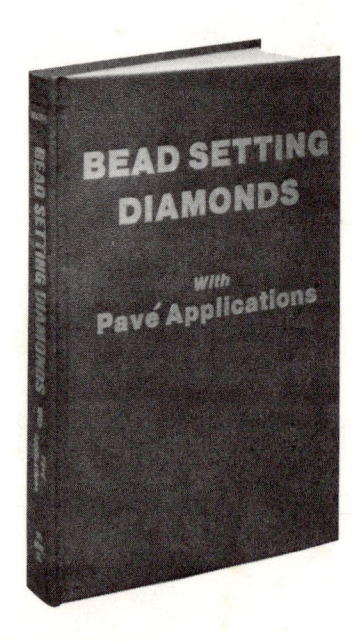

Raising beads and bright cutting simplified

Over 250 photographs of actual bead setting tasks

Self-paced — Easy to follow — Step by Step

Pave' diamond setting procedures pictorially illustrated

Includes detailed line drawings to clarify each phase of bead setting

Contains advanced pave' setting techniques

"Excellent reference source"

"192 informative pages"

YOUR COST
$29⁹⁵

ADVANCED INSTRUCTIONAL BOOK FOR BEAD SETTING DIAMONDS!

CONTENTS

SECTION I — TOOL PREPARATION AND MAINTENANCE

Introduction........................3
1 Tool List 4
(Description and purpose)
2 Heat Treating Steel 21
Annealing.........................22
Hardening 23
Tempering........................23
Forging 24
3 Graver Preparation 25
Assembling Graver and Handle 26
Shaping Gravers 28
Sharpening Gravers 30
4 Making A Beading Tool...........32
Option NO.1—by Heat Treating......32
Option NO.2—by Forging............35

SECTION II — THE BEAD SETTING PROCEDURE

Introduction........................39
1 Inspect The Mounting 41
(Checklist)
2 Design A Layout..................45
Designing A Symmetric Layout 46
Designing A Freeform Layout 48
3 Drill The Holes 53
Indent Center Points 53
How A Drill Works 53
Drilling Holes 54
4 Taper Bore The Holes 57
5 Cut The Bearing 60
Sequence Of Bearing Cutting........60
Selecting The Correct Size Bur 63
Cutting A Bearing Into A
  Shallow Plate....................65
6 Seat The Diamond 66
Clean The Bearing 67
Clean The Diamond................67
Seat The Diamond 68
7 Secure The Diamond 70
Raising Beads 70
Raising One Bead Onto
  Two Diamonds 72
Securing A Diamond With
  Minimum Beads 73
8 Engrave Excess Metal.............75
9 Shape The Beads.................77
Using A Beading Tool 77
Alternate Means To Shape Beads 78
10 Bright Cut The Metal............81
Polishing The Tip Of A Flat Graver...81
Bright Cutting 83
Alternate Means Of Bright Cutting....85

SECTION III — BEAD SETTING APPLICATIONS

Introduction........................91
1 Star Setting......................93
An introductory application to bead setting. The importance and effects of engraving is stressed.
2 Square Plate 100
This Segment details the basic bead setting procedure of setting a single diamond into a square plate.
3 Triangle Plate 107
A triangle plate is introduced to progress to a geometric shape and procedure variations.
4 Hexagon Plate 113
The Skills of raising beads and bright cutting are exercised in this application to elaborate a symmetric design.
5 Marquis Plate 119
Bead setting mulitple diamonds into a marquis plate demonstrate smaller diamonds can be arranged to resemble a larger and fancier diamond.
6 Bead Setting Diamonds In A Row..125
The basic procedure of setting a single diamond into a square plate is repeated in a serial order to illustrate setting a row of diamonds.
7 Bead Setting Diamonds
  Into A Curve....................133
The Fundamental procedures of raising beads and bright cutting are varied to bead set diamonds into circular paths.

SECTION IV — ADVANCED PAVE' SETTING

Introduction.......................144
1 Square Cluster 145
Bead setting nine diamonds into a square cluster is illustrated in this segment to introduce the formation of pave' diamond setting.
2 Round Cluster 153
Seven diamonds are bead set into a round cluster to show that a group of diamonds can be set to resemble one large diamond.
3 Oval Cluster 162
Unequal sizes of diamonds are bead set into a uniform arrangement to stress the significance of careful planning during the layout phase.
4 Pear Cluster 162
Problem solving is intensified in this segment to show the importance of acquiring basic bead setting skills.
5 Freestyle Cluster 178
A classic example of pave' bead setting is presented to demonstrate unique variations of the bead setting procedure.